Defining Edge

Practice Management Strategies

A Programme of Innovative Strategies for Improving Accounting Firm Management, Marketing and Profitability

**Your Coach
Mark Lloydbottom**

Defining Edge Practice Management Strategies

Mark Lloydbottom, FCA

First Published 2009 by Marrho Limited © 2009

Reprint August 2009
Reprint 2013

This book and the accompanying CDs and DVDs are published by Marrho Limited. No responsibility for loss occasioned to any person acting or refraining from action as a result of any material in this publication can be accepted by the author or publisher.

All rights reserved. No part of this publication, CD or DVD may be reproduced, stored in a retrieval system, or transmitted, in any form or by any means, electronic, mechanical, photocopy, recording or otherwise, without prior permission of the publisher.

Typeset by Fleur Isbell

Printed and bound in Great Britain By T.J. International Ltd

Contents

    i.   Your Coach's Track Record: Mark Lloydbottom

   ii.   Coaches letter

  iii.   Introduction

1st session: Welcome to the training ground

1. Our accounting firm model – how you can increase profits
2. Your personal development

2nd session: We have clients to serve – What do they expect?

1. Meeting your clients face-to-face – let's look at numbers and value
2. Leveraging your client meetings – the value of a clear agenda
3. And….action – the client planning meeting
4. Outstanding service – the rewards can be substantial

3rd session: Quality and value – The keys to clients coming back and making recommendations

1. Your report card – raising your score performance
2. Managing your 'moments of truth'
3. Enhancing the value of what you deliver
4. Projecting a high quality image

4th session: The billing canvas – Setting the scene

1. Billing – an introduction
2. Billing myths – surely they can't be true
3. Top line management

4. Setting prices – realisation and value under the microscope

5. Discussing prices with clients – agreeing the fee

5th session: Delivering results – Getting paid what you're worth

1. 21 ways to improve your billing

2. Avoiding write downs

3. Setting the right standard charge out rates

4. Guerilla warfare

5. The job is not finished until the cheque clears the bank

6th session – Marketing – Your next generation of clients

1. Marketing – an introduction

2. Marketing planning

3. Core marketing strategies

4. Relationship and reputation building

5. A range of marketing strategies that work

And finally...

A record of those who have helped me develop as an individual, a business owner and consultant.

Defining Edge
Practice Management Strategies

You coach's track record: Mark Lloydbottom FCA, CPC

Mark specialises in management planning and strategy for accounting firms. His programmes and consulting are based on over 25 years experience as a practitioner and consultant. He has worked with professional service firms in seven foreign countries and has lectured throughout Europe and North America.

Mark was a practitioner for 16 years starting his own practice in Bristol in 1978. He is the founder of the Association of British Independent Accounting Firms, Practice Track and PracticeWEB and he has also served on various committees with the Institute of Chartered Accountants including the 2005 Working Party.

Mark has worked closely with leading firms in the US including Practice Development Institute based in Chicago, BizActions based in Maryland, AccountingWEB in Indianapolis and Faust Management Corporation in San Diego. He also works with a number of the UK's leading accounting firm associations and accounting institutes.

Mark is the co-author of Clients4Life published by the Institute of Chartered Accountants of Scotland.

He is devoted to researching and identifying strategies to enable accounting firms to build the top and bottom line. He achieves this by delivering high quality consulting and lecturing and remains PracticeWEB's principal author maintaining the site content for more than 700 accounting firms.

Apart from business interests, Mark enjoys Mountain Biking, is an active Church member, trustee of two charities and a director of Crown Financial Ministries.

He is always available for making speeches and consulting on firm management, strategies for improving client service and for reducing lock up. To discuss how he can assist you please contact:

Mark Lloydbottom:
t: (44)07767 872 278
e: mark@marklloydbottom.com
w: www.marklloydbottom.com

Coaches letter

At the heart of this programme there are six hours with me as your coach. What is my goal? No, it is not to persuade you to agree with me on all of my analysis, strategies and tactics. I was a practitioner for only fifteen years – you may already have more experience than me. You may have grown your business faster or be more profitable than I was. In any event you will have your own way of approaching the areas at the core of every practice – owners, staff, clients, service and business management. You are unlikely to have invested in this programme unless you have a business you want to improve; that's my goal in the six hours we spend together.

So, please feel free to have an alternative point of view to mine. I am only your coach and I know there is more than one way to score a goal. If you disagree with anything you hear, you must know what you believe to be right for you and your firm. You may hear something that does not apply to you – I trust you will not have to wait long before you find something that does.

I started my own practice in 1976 and was managing partner for fifteen years. I am grateful to all those who helped me develop my abilities to run the business – firstly there were clients and staff. Secondly, I learnt so much from working with Mike Platt, now the author of Inside Public Accounting in the US and my consulting colleague Dave Cottle. There are of course others who I have listed at the end of this manual and to all I have met and worked with I give you my thanks.

While building Practice Track I developed a set of audio tapes called *Going For Growth* and *Managing Growth*. The content of *Defining Edge* Practice Management Strategies bears little or no resemblance to those early programmes. Some 20 years later much has changed – I have learnt more and volumes have been written about accounting firm management that has shaped my thinking and understanding of what constitutes best practice.

If you have the DVD then you may well watch this on a DVD player or TV – if the latter and you are watching on your home TV, you will find there is probably no one else who will wish to watch! You may be using one or more of the training sessions as an integral part of your firm's training. In any event, I recommend you read all of this manual as in six hours of programmes which is what you have acquired I do not try to cover all the content. Equally, do not read this manual without listening to or watching the discs as there are stories I tell that are not captured in the manual. Equally there is material in the manual that is not on the disks. I regard this as a self-study manual for it is easier to assimilate the content on paper than listen to me for too long. The self-study content in particular includes the module on marketing planning (module 2 session 6) and part of module 5 session 3 on setting charge rates.

When I started my practice there was little management material that I could access and so much of my early life as a business owner revolved around trial and error. I trust the content of *Defining Edge* Practice Management Strategies enables you to learn from others who have been there and done it.

Enjoy *Defining Edge* Practice Management Strategies – may it challenge and help you to improve your life

Mark Lloydbottom
Mark Lloydbottom
Your Coach for a Season

Introduction

How satisfied are you with the health of your practice? Are you winning new clients? Are you feeling happy about the state of play in the practice? Are you happy? Are your staff happy? Are your clients satisfied with your service? Are you the best accountant in town?

Looks like a lot of questions. You should expect *Defining Edge* Practice Management Strategies to ask and answer a lot of questions. It may not answer all your questions, but I trust that it provides a range of strategies that you will able to adopt and adapt so as to improve what you do and how you do it. Treat our time together as a health check. How are you doing in each area? What should you change? What can you do differently?

In the twenty first century the accounting marketplace is more competitive than ever. Clients now have more information available to them about professional firms – and prospects are far less likely to make decisions based only on a recommendation.

If clients and prospects see no other difference between you and your competitors they *must* decide on price because that's the only difference they can see!

The more you try to become like everyone else, the less you become like you.

Your biggest asset is your uniqueness – especially your unique advisory proposition (UAP). What knowledge do you have that enables you to be different?

To stand out from the crowd you need to provide outstanding services – and outstanding service.

This coaching programme will help you: (partial list)

- Look at your firm and its performance through our LUBRM financial model
- Work with your clients and not on them
- Position yourself as your clients' number one expert and adviser
- Identify your uniqueness and position yourself head and shoulders above your competitors
- Ensure you provide the services – and the value clients need
- Upgrade client loyalty and transform clients into advocates for your firm
- Improve job satisfaction for yourself and your employees
- Increase profitability and firm value by working smarter, not harder
- Identify clients who truly need what you can do for them
- Develop richer, trusting relationships with clients
- Communicate your full range of services in ways that improve your services to clients
- Ensure a firm-wide commitment to outstanding service
- Raise your standard charge out rates if needed

- Charge more for those engagements that justify a higher price
- Learn the tools to implement specific value pricing ideas
- Collect your invoices sooner, with fewer bad debts
- Upgrade the profitability of serving B and C clients
- Avoid price disputes and, if they occur, handle misunderstandings in a mutually agreeable and profitable manner.

How to make Defining Edge Practice Management Strategies work for you

- Don't wait to discuss these ideas with everyone in your firm. Delay leads to forgetfulness. Act immediately on the most relevant ideas you find. The sooner you act, the better you internalise new ideas and remember them.
- Read books on accounting firm management, marketing, client service, pricing and invoicing.
- Expect results. Approach *Defining Edge* Practice Management Strategies with an open attitude. When you go to a department store, not everything in the store will interest you, but *something* in that store will. Most seminars are the same way. *Defining Edge* is like a tool kit. Every job you undertake around your home does not require every tool in your kit. Sometimes you need only the pliers and a screwdriver. But it's nice to have that set of metric wrenches or a Phillips screwdriver when the specific job that needs them comes along.
- To get the most from your coach, take my ideas and tailor them to your situation. Keep a pen handy (assuming you are not driving) as you hear things or read ideas that are of interest to you. When something you hear or read sparks an idea, write it down right then before you forget it. Follow this advice and you will invest your time and not just spend it. Somewhere in *Defining Edge* Practice Management Strategies, you will find a few really valuable ideas that will enhance your practice.

Some service challenges

- The purpose of a business is to meet the needs of its customers. There is an emphasis in *Defining Edge* Practice Management Strategies on recognising and meeting those needs, getting paid for doing so and finding other clients who need your services.
- If there is something a client needs that you are qualified to provide but you do not provide it, you are not serving that client well.
- Twenty-six out of every twenty-seven people who have a bad experience with a firm won't complain. Why not? Because they expect little or no satisfaction if they do. What's scary about this is that most people with a bad experience don't come back. You may hear complaints from a few clients, but you certainly won't hear the majority.
- Even worse, on average, a person who has been let down by their accountant tells

9 – 10 other people – and one out of every eight grumblers spreads the bad news to 20 or more people – could some clients be badmouthing you? Yes, if your service quality score is not high enough.

This may seem like bad news, but it's actually good news for you and your firm. Why? Because people who switch their business to a competing firm are five times more likely to cite poor service as the reason than they are price or quality.

Key point: In other words, the problem is not price but service – and service can be fixed without spending a fortune.

Here's some more good news:

- Firms that score highly on relative quality can charge prices 20 – 50 percent higher than the average firm in their community can – and still gain market share at the expense of lower-quality firms.
- Firms with superior quality have operating costs about the same as the lower-quality firms. This, combined with higher fees, makes them up to *twice as profitable as firms with low quality.*

What this means for you and your firm

The greatest key to a successful professional practice can be summed up in three words: *outstanding client service.*

It's the best-kept secret in the accounting world!

Providing outstanding service to clients is – or should be – the number one priority for all accountants.

Poor quality service is the principal cause of losing clients to competitors.

Can you change this? Yes; you just have to know what to do differently. And one of the things you must do differently is to work *with* your clients instead of just working *on* your clients.

Today, the only constant is change. The economy is tough. Competition is intense; other accountants and even non-accountants are actively pursuing your clients. In this environment, giving outstanding client service is not just a competitive weapon; it's a survival essential!

There are firms that thrive in today's marketplace environment, firms that grow in flat or depressed markets, firms that outstrip their competition, and firms that enhance both the quality and the quantity of their services to clients while providing a satisfying work environment for their personnel.

Behind every star performer there is a coach

Think of any famous sporting personality. In the past you might have thought of Jane Torvill or George Best. Today it might be Wayne Rooney or Laura Robson. These 'stars' have even higher profiles and earn considerably more, but one thing they all have in common – in addition to their natural skill – *is a commitment to practice*. For them practice is an indispensable commitment both for maintaining and enhancing their skills.

Typically, their practice sessions are led by a coach, whose experience and wisdom enables them to focus on where they can improve – and how to do so.

Permit me to be *your* coach as we look at how you view your performance as an accountant, business owner and client adviser. We will look at what you do, your knowledge, your capabilities, your firm and a wide range of areas that together comprise your marketplace proposition, the value you deliver to the community and the profit you generate from the business.

As coaches should, I encourage and challenge you to think and act differently. I am mindful that you will have an alternative view on some of the matters we discuss. You don't have to agree with everything I say. The only end result that counts is for you to identify with what you believe is right and can commit to implement.

Some of our key concepts

Accounting firms provide three types of service.

- *Specialist/niche services*
- Extension and advisory services
- Compliance services

Specialist/niche services

These services are key to your firm's USP (Unique Sales Proposition). They set the firm apart and provide opportunities to promote service(s) not offered by other local firms. These services may be to a particular service sector or they may be a specialism(s) that can be delivered across a range of clients, e.g. estate planning, financial services and so on.

With specialist/niche services the firm commits to offer service(s) beyond the traditional compliance offering. These services entail special expertise as well as a dedication to service delivery. Such expertise is a specialisation developed to enable the firm to have a robust commitment to the delivery of services directly relevant to a particular industry or specialist service. Specialist training needs to be developed and maintained and this may include additional staff training, increased research and studying as well as networking and other time commitments. These services have marketplace appeal and great fee potential.

In *Defining Edge* Practice Management Strategies we do not specifically cover the scope of the development of specialist services, but the principles I discuss apply.

Extension and advisory services

These are services related to what a client could or should do in the future. They relate to future planning and *may* encompass knowledge gained during compliance service engagements.

Advisory services are not exclusively driven by compliance expertise and are wider in scope as they are not necessarily solely dependent on your knowledge.

Evidence shows that not all firms have succeeded in introducing such advisory services. We will look at how you can develop your ability to offer what I prefer to call 'extension services'.

Extension services are those services that clients automatically associate as being provided by their accountant. These services extend the service into the present operating environment of the client.

Compliance services

We owe a debt of gratitude to governments, tax authorities, and regulatory bodies whose requirements bring clients back to firms year after year.

Let us look at the two primary roles the accountant plays in service delivery – expert and adviser. Some accountants major on one role with limited incursions into the other, while others specialise in only one.

Your role as an expert

We use accountant and expert as interchangeable terms. We regard all your compliance services as being delivered by you as expert, as clients recognise you as the expert in these fields.

Your technical expertise and knowledge of compliance-related planning services position you as an expert. You have extensive up-to-date knowledge and can provide solutions to your clients' problems. You tell clients what is best for them and recommend actions to take.

Although you could view this as advice, in the context of compliance services we regard such advice as being integral to the compliance service itself, and not a separate advisory service. Indeed, if you are *not* adding advice to your compliance service offering, you are not serving your client well.

With compliance services, you remain in control of the process and have the expertise to meet the clients' needs – you are the expert.

Your role as an adviser

The adviser role differs from that of an expert, although in practice there is to some, perhaps, no clear line between them.

We will look at the principle differences between expert and adviser and present the case for you to extend your advisory services. In fact, we conclude that if you do *not* offer these (extension and advisor) services you are *failing* to fully serve your clients.

We might add that expanding your role allows you to enjoy a more rewarding professional life.

Can you be an expert only? Yes. If you do not provide niche/specialist services or compliance services with minimal advice.

Can you be an adviser only? No. You advance your position as adviser from your compliance services. With compliance services your primary role is that of expert.

Can you be expert/adviser? Yes. We will look at this later.

Visible time

We focus on the 'visible' time you spend with your clients. This is your one-on-one, face-to-face meeting time. We will look at why and how you should increase this time. Conversely the time you do not spend with clients we regard, as 'desktop' or non-visible time.

Outstanding quality

Along with many other terms such as *excellence, reengineering,* and *downsizing, quality* was a buzzword during the last quarter of the 20th century. Whereas some of the other terms might have fallen out of currency, *quality* remains a cornerstone of professional service and a key driver in success with clients and firm growth. Quality has many facets, and references to it are woven throughout *Defining Edge* Practice Management Strategies.

I believe that quality should be not just *superior*, but *outstanding*.

Important acknowledgement

For over 20 years it has been my privilege to work with Dave Cottle, a consultant to accounting firms in the USA. When we first met he presented a seminar entitled *Double Your Money* in cities across the UK. Subsequently, Dave developed a number of seminars in order to meet our need to present new material aimed at helping firms improve their management and profitability. This manual has been enhanced by adopting some of Dave's ideas. We have shared ideas and materials over the years and I am grateful to him for allowing me to incorporate some of his material in this manual. I wish to place on record that I value Dave's ability to craft a manual and seminar so that the ideas are easy to understand. Dave's website includes a range of the other books and materials he has authored.

Let's get started

With my introduction complete, it is time to get started.

Welcome to the training ground – 1st session

Module 1
Our accounting firm model

I was first introduced to the LUBRM model by Dave Cottle (my co-author of Clients 4Life) who had first seen this when studying the Weiner Worksheet, developed by Ron Weiner of New York. I find this provides valuable insight into the core model of how you can look at an accounting firm and the keys to how you can take management decisions that improve firm profitability. So often management material is adopted by many and I wish to give credit where it is due.

The four types of management activity

Our firm revenues are derived from our productivity (doing the work) and our pricing (the amount we charge).

Our net income is the revenue, less the cost of earning that revenue (cost management), less the write downs taken (client management).

Therefore, in generating a profit firms engage in four types of management activity:

1. Productivity
2. Pricing
3. Cost management
4. Client management

These four management activities combine and provide five keys that influence the quantum of the bottom line.

The five keys to firm profitability

Long term keys:

1. Leverage (L)
2. Margin (M)

Short term keys:

3. Billing rate (B)
4. Utilisation (U)
5. Realisation (R)

1st:1 | Our accounting firm model

Defining these terms

Leverage (L)

Leverage is the total number of professional and support people in the firm divided by the number of firm owners.

Example: a firm with 9 owners and 19 professional and support staff has a total of 28 personnel and a leverage of 3.1 Thus an owner has responsibility for managing himself and three staff members.

Margin (M)

Margin is the economic net profit percentage on net fees.

| Margin | = | Economic net profit on net fees / Net fees |

Billing rate (B)

The firm billing rate is the weighted average standard billing rate per hour. It is calculated by dividing the standard fees – the total billing at standard rates – by the total chargeable hours.

| Billing rate | = | Standard fees / Total chargeable hours |

Utlisation (U)

Utilisation is the average annual chargeable hours per person.

Example:	In the last twelve months – Total chargeable hours	38,910
	Total personnel	28
	Utilisation =	1,390

Realisation (R)

Realisation is the net fees billed (after write downs and write ups) expressed as a percentage of standard fees.

Example: An engagement with a standard fee of £10,000 is billed for £9,000. Realisation is £9,000 divided into £10,000 = 90%

Our accounting firm model

LUBRM Case Studies				
	Firm 1	Firm 2	Firm 3	Firm 4
Partners	9	8	6	8
Total personnel	28	52	106	60
Leverage (L)	3.1	6.5	17.7	7.5
Chargeable hours	38,910	53,398	109,866	89,946
Utilisation (U)	1,390	1,027	1,036	1,499
Standard fees	1,945,500	2,242,716	7,910,352	4,857,084
Billing rate per hours (B)	£50	£42	£72	£54
Net Fees	1,907,563	2,164,221	5,932,764	4,837,656
Realisation % (R)	98.1%	96.5%	75.0%	99.6%
Net Income	654,294	664,416	1,370,468	1,794,770
Margin % (M)	34.3%	30.7%	23.1%	37.1%
Net Income Per Partner (NIPP)	£72,699	£83,052	£228,411	£224,346

The short-term keys provide the immediate opportunity to increase the firm's profitability. Let us look at some examples.

What is the bottom line effect for firm 1 of:

An increase in utilisation:

	Hours
Currently	1,390
Increase to	1,440
An increase of	50

Revenue increase of (28 x 50) hours = 1,400 hours @ £50 = £70,000 @ 98.1% = **£68,670**

Increase in NIPP = **£7,630 (10.5%)**

An increase in the hourly billing rate

	£
Billing rate at present	£50
Increase to	£51
Increase of	£1

1st:1 | Our accounting firm model

Total increase of £1 for all hours, assuming all realised = **£38,910**

Increase in NIPP = **£4,323 (5.9%)**

An increase in realisation: %

Realisation at present	98.1
Increase to	99.1
Increase of	1.0

Revenue increase of 1% of £1,945,500, assuming all realised = **£19,455**

Increase in NIPP of **– £2,162 (3%)**

Some strategies for improving the short term keys

1. Utilisation

	Strategy	Already Implemented	Consider	To Action
1	Set targets for all chargeable staff, including partners.			
2	Capture time daily. Those firms who capture time daily report an increase in chargeable hours of between 4-6%.			
3	Use the "50 minute hour."			
4	Consider using the "15 minute hour."			
5	Eliminate any areas of firm practise that could cause partners and staff not to charge time. For example, if there is a strong firm culture on high realisation, certain individuals may conclude that it would be wiser to avoid some of this pressure by not recording all the hours worked.			

		Already Implemented	Consider	To Action
6	Develop a structured programme for client meetings by partners and managers. Implementation should be monitored by each individual.			
7	Monitor utilisation regularly and establish why specific time goals are not being met.			
8	Feedback chargeable hour information both budgeted and actual to all partners and staff for both information and competitive purposes.			
9	Don't allow partners to 'donate' time to clients.			
10	Review your scheduling process and determine if it can be improved.			

We will look again at some of these in our fifth training session.

2. Realisation

	Strategy	Already Implemented	Consider	To Action
1	Bill more promptly, while the tears of appreciation are still moist in client's eyes.			
2	Send interim bills.			
3	Ensure that problems encountered on field work are raised with the client immediately. In this instance the interaction with the client establishes who assumes responsibility for solving the problem and how much this will cost above the 'normal' fee if it is agreed that your firm is responsible for solving the problem.			
4	Be careful with fixed fees unless you are sure that you will generate at least the required realisation rate.			

1st:1 | Our accounting firm model

5	Don't schedule assignments wall-to-wall. Allow time for the person in charge of the engagement to complete the work so that the bill can be raised without delay.			
6	Introduce a firm policy whereby a bill giving rise to a realisation of less than 85% of standard has to have second partner approval.			
7	Introduce a policy where no realisation of less than 85% is made without a face-to-face client meeting.			
8	Use the firm's best billers. Arrange training and have the best billers train those who need to improve their billing skills.			
9	Who is responsible for billing? It is likely that the engagement manager may have a better knowledge of the work input. Delegating billing to managers normally results in higher realisation. Managers may be future firm owners – allow them the opportunity to practice and hone their billing skills.			
10	Establish firm realisation goals. Monitor regularly and give prompt feedback to those concerned.			
11	Reduce price sensitivity by exceeding clients' expectations. Look at what is provided from the client's perspective. The client assumes technical expertise; he or she expects, and is entitled to, more than that.			
12	Beware of the anchor of the last years' bill.			

We will look again at some of these in our fifth training session.

3. Billing Rate

	Strategy	Already Implemented	Consider	To Action
1	Do you have the right approach to setting charge rates?			
2	Consider raising your charge rates by three times the rate of inflation for firm owners and twice for staff. This increases the 'time on', *not* the amount you bill the client.			
3	Introduce different charge rates where higher value work is undertaken. A premium for work that has greater value is a generally accepted principle.			
4	Consider raising fees on your most aggravating clients. If you lose them as a result, you may be better off.			
5	Who are your worst clients? Who do staff think are your worst clients? Consider 'firing' the worst clients thus freeing up more time with the best clients.			
6	When concerns are raised about the quality of service provided, don't compromise on fees – aim to provide an enhanced service instead.			
7	Select clients carefully – some clients will always complain about fees and you don't need this type of client. Even clients with potential for high fees may not be worth it in the long run.			

We will look again at some of these in our fifth training session.

1st:1 | Our accounting firm model

Time: an investment and one of your raw materials

Investment definition: 'To lay out with an expectation of gain'.

1. Investment time with clients – both you and the client are looking for a return

2. Investment time for you and the firm – CPD, holidays, marketing and so on

I find it interesting that the range of chargeable and total hours for firm owners varies greatly. Allow me to illustrate my point by reviewing a few areas. In looking at some of these the key performance indicators I recognise I am addressing my peers, who in some cases have enjoyed a longer career than my 15 years as an accounting firm owner. However I have spent many years consulting with accounting firms and these insights are gleaned from my experiences both as a practitioner and consultant. My knowledge has been enhanced by other consultants and books written by many distinguished authors. The purpose of this programme is not to produce a book like Clients 4Life with its 400 pages, but to look at a number of key areas that, to some extent, revolve around the LUBRM model. We will look at other areas of performance and owner input in the forthcoming modules.

Time on: What is your firm input?

When I started as a trainee accountant it seemed that jobs lasted for either one week or a multiple of weeks. While that was many years ago, I was interested to find that my youngest son, now training to be an accountant has his time occupied with audits that last one week, two weeks or three. In that situation completing a time sheet with 37 ½ hours is easy because it is all chargeable to one client. Moving the clock forward to when I became a manager I recall that at the end of the week my time sheet had some full days at clients and others when my time sheet had time charged to two or three clients. Roll the clock forward to when I was in practice and there were times when I struggled to account for five hours, let alone seven and a half. My daily time sheet might have 20 client entries, but some were for only 10 minutes.

So, what does the 'time on' scene look like today? Let's start by looking at some 'facts'.

Firm owners' time is not normally confined to 9-5. Many practitioners are working more than 40 hours a week, even though not evidenced by their time sheet. Consider:

1. Not every partner records his time fully

2. Some partners find the prospect of their time recording demotivating

3. In the same firm there are inconsistencies in the way partners complete their time reporting

4. Surveys show that when total time is captured total hours vary from 2,200-2,800 hours per annum, per owner, with an average of 2,450.

5. Inter firm surveys show that owner chargeable hours per annum vary from 600 to 1,350 hours with an average of 1,150 per owner.

6. By deduction some partners have 'non chargeable' time in excess of their chargeable time.

Your time 'dustbin' and downtime

If you commit to capturing all your time, it is inevitable that there will be time that you cannot account for. Beware the trap of 'admin' or whatever other dustbin you are accustomed to writing up your time to. Use a downtime account.

Improving work profitability

	Strategy	Already Implemented	Consider	To Action
1	When to prepare the budget. Prepare next year's budget when this year's work has been concluded.			
2	Include a 'Job Postscript' (pg10)			
3	Depreciate the job budget – most firms tend to accumulate time.			
4	Involve the client in the budgeting process (pg11).			

1st:1 | Our accounting firm model

Job Postscript		
Client: _____ P/E _____		
Prepared By: _____ On: _____		
For Next Year's A.I.C.		
These are the three keys you need to know to succeed on this job:		
1	*Always arrive early*	
2	*Do not waste time chatting with staff*	
3	*Ask for M.D.'s accounts*	
	These are the three keys you need to know to beat the time elapsed on this year's job	
1	*Make sure client keeps supplier's statements*	
2	*Watch for client caused problems in sales ledger*	
3	*Don't waste time trying to balance the purchase control*	
	I wish you every success	

Client Budgeting – up to £x million					
Section	Work to Do	Value	Comment	Min Hrs	Hours
A	Accounts – Trial Balance			15	
B	Analytical Review			5	
C	Planning			4	
D	Points for Review			3	
E	Fixed assets			8	
F	Expenditure/Creditors			15	
G	Directors/Partners			10	
H	Stock/WIP			15	
I	Revenue/Debtors			15	
J	Cash and Bank			6	
K	Taxation			10	
L	Share Capital			2	
M	Journals			5	
N	Detailed Nominal			20	
Other	Accounting work				
	Total hours				
	Average cost @ £____ p.h.				£
				£	
	Partner review			300	
	Client business and management advice			250	
	Company taxation			250	
	Expenses			0	
	Personal taxation			300	
	Budgeted time costs				£
	Agreed fee				£
	Initial meetings and file set up				£

Advantages of the client budgeting approach

1. It is we, not I compiling the quote

2. It enables you to manage the prospect's expectations

3. It enables you to capture the £s you will audit, which helps when the question of 'variation orders' arises

4. Provides opportunity to agree with the prospect what services are required

5. Enables you to identify an unreasonable/undesirable client

6. It is a client-friendly and engaging process

Owners bottom line

Owners are required, without being reminded, to be active and successful in the following areas:

1. Achieving chargeable and total (investment) hours

2. Maximising visibility with clients

3. Maintaining and enhancing personal capabilities

4. Achieving target for client meetings

5. Engaging with professional referrals

6. Winning new clients

7. Maximising service opportunities with existing clients

8. Billing and keeping WIP to ____% (target – default – 12 percent)

9. Collecting and keeping debtors to ____% (target – default 22 percent)

10. Achieving realisation of not less than ____% (target – default – 85 percent)

1st session

Module 2
Your personal development

Question 1: What have you learned in the last year to make yourself more valuable to your clients?

Never regard studying as a duty, but as the enviable opportunity to learn to know the liberating influence of beauty in the realm of the spirit for your own personal joy and to the profit of the community to which your later works belong.
Albert Einstein

Question 2: As you develop your skills in the next five years, what is going to be your special claim to fame? What is your personal strategic plan? If there were a ladder inside your brain, would you still be on the same rung as last year looking at the same views, or would you have climbed higher and be looking at new vistas? What have you learned in the last year that has heightened your skills and knowledge and made you more valuable to your clients?

Your core competency – still up-to-date?

No doubt you attend all the courses and read all the press releases and technical updates that ensure you are up-to-date. However, with ever-increasing legislation, regulation and technology there can be a time when keeping up-to-date is not top of the list, or maybe even on the list. This applies especially if you have others around who are not co-owners and whose job responsibility it is to be up-to-date. When you look ahead at the rest of your career, what services and advice would you like to offer? What opportunities might you have?

Some practitioners, especially those who are sole owners, are required to keep abreast in most general practice areas but then outsource engagements where specialist advice is required. They keep an eye on change and make it their business to be in the know. Some practitioners have specialised either in an industry or a particular service. How do you wish to extend your own knowledge? What can you learn and then practice?

Initiating a new personal development regime pays dividends

As *knowledge workers* we have a virtually unlimited capacity to learn and the opportunity to engage clients who want and need that expertise. The analogy with following a physical fitness regime is obvious. It takes commitment to studying and not to be deterred or give up. If you have started but your commitment has waned, resolve to resume.

As you enhance your knowledge this can become your *Unique Advisory Proposition* (UAP). The quality and incisiveness of your advice maintains your position as a valued adviser, especially with those *B* clients for whom you wish to deliver more visible time and who have previously viewed your service as more *product* than *service*.

Competition among accountants is intense and with clients unable to easily compare one firm's tax or accounts service with another, the UAP can be an important factor in the decision as to which firm to appoint as accountant. The UAP is certainly prominent in client retention and satisfaction.

Technology has further empowered governmental and regulatory organisations to prescribe the formats in which we submit returns. Uniformity it seems is now obligatory, but the drive for uniformity has resulted in forms, formats and procedures that are not always easy for clients to understand or follow.

A starting point for extending your ability to tell stories

Activities or processes that work for some do not necessarily work for others. By their nature, stories that you find in books tend to be about 'famous' people, famous organisations or about acclaimed subjects or by well known authors. Publishers and bookstores sell the books that people want to buy and so it is often these well-known companies that abide in the memory that we can relate to and learn from. We can all learn from well publicised success or failure corporate stories and the principles they highlight. An extract from my top ten include:

1. Coca-Cola

During the 1970s Coca Cola's dominance in the marketplace was challenged head on by Pepsi Cola and the 'Pepsi Challenge'. Consumers were asked to compare the taste of Coke with Pepsi and expressed a clear preference for Pepsi. Pepsi's US market share increased from 6 to 14 percent. Even Coca-Cola's own research indicated similar results. This resulted in Coca-Cola undertaking extensive research in 10 major markets to ascertain whether customers would accept a new taste.

Coca-Cola invested $4 million in mass tasting of a range of new coca-cola tastes. Armed with the research results, the company was confident their new drink would be a success and so they launched a new flavour of Coca-Cola.

Soon, the company was besieged with angry phone calls and 40,000 letters expressing disapproval of the new taste. To begin with, the calls and feedback were dismissed as 'relatively insignificant' but after complaints from half a million consumers, the company realised they had made a monumental mistake. As a result, the company was forced to reintroduce old Coke as Coca-Cola Classic© and rebranded the new Coke, New Coke©.

There were those that argued that the strategy had been to boost sales, but the company denied this claiming that it wasn't smart enough to come up with a plan like that. New Coke disappeared shortly after.

As an addendum to this story, some 20 years later the company sought to launch its Dasani bottled water in Europe. Launches of the product in France and Germany were stymied when press reports rumoured that the 'fresh' water came from a water pipe in south east London and that despite a sophisticated purification process the water was found to contain high levels of a chemical linked to cancer. The outcome? The complete withdrawal of Dasani from the European marketplace.

Lessons to be learned: Market research and planning do not guarantee the right decision. Be careful when tampering with a traditional image. Major changes are often better introduced alongside the present.

Note: I include here brief summaries of some of the lessons to be learned from other well known corporate stories. These stories are told in the appendix A of Clients 4Life.

2. Euro Disney

Lessons to be learned: Do not be complacent, do not assume that optimistic forecasts will be achieved when dealing with new markets and new marketplaces, do not overprice even when in a monopoly situation.

3. Hoover

Lessons learned: Have a well thought-out strategy that makes economic sense. Where was the voice of the accountant in the development of the promotional plan? Today, a spreadsheet with a range of 'what-if' scenarios would quickly reveal the extent to which a promotion of this nature would incur losses. You don't need rocket science to determine that this strategy would result in disaster from the outset. It is important for those who own a business to maintain an involvement in key strategic planning areas. Responsibility can be delegated, but not ultimate accountability. However, when mistakes are made take care how you resolve these to avoid excessive costs. Failure to respond to new technology and innovate can ultimately result in a businesses demise in the marketplace. Price was not an issue for US consumers. I used to play tennis with two members of Dyson's R&D department, while recovering from a closely fought doubles game one evening, I was told that there were always 300 products that R&D were evaluating in that company.

4. Ratners

Lessons learned: Never think or speak negatively about your company's products or services, or indeed the staff. Ensure you communicate clearly and appropriately to staff and customers if and when you face your 'crap moment'. Curiously, as a footnote Gerald Ratner sought to launch an online jewellery business and his right to do so using the Ratner name was challenged. So, maybe a brand can recover from almost anything? Other company's that have endured public concerns about their products include Perrier, whose water supply in 1990 was found to have traces of benzene – a chemical linked with cancer.

In Clients 4Life I include the full stories and lessons learned from looking at the corporate stories of:
- Continental Airlines
- EasyJet

- Harley Davidson
- IBM
- Virgin
- Wal-Mart

Out of the box personal development

What other opportunities or challenges do you have? I know a number of partners who have extended their business advisory capabilities by studying for an MBA. Was this *thinking outside the box*? It started as this because the thought had not previously occurred to them, but it became *living outside the box* when they committed to the programme and then moved on, with their partners' approval, to integrate their enhanced capabilities into services to clients. They recognised there was another level they could move to and were determined to extend their advisory knowledge so they could create new 'moments of magic' with their clients.

Over the years I have learned to advance my skills and knowledge by learning to study other consultants. In the accounting profession I have been privileged to learn from Dr Gerry Faust who taught me the stages of corporate development through his lifecycle model; Allan Koltin of the Practice Development Institute, Dave Cottle, my co-author and those accounting firms who have allowed me to work with them as they seek to progress their business. In addition I have also studied the books authored by consultants such as Warren Bennis, Stephen Covey, Peter Drucker, Michael Gerber, Gary Hammel, Michael Hammer, Charles Handy, Rosabeth Moss Kanter, Tom Peters and Michael Porter.

As accountants we should develop a growing body of client-relevant knowledge. Imagine your mind being analysed. What do you find when looking at your bank of knowledge? What percentage of the information you have available to pass on is out-of-date? How much of your knowledge is current and reinforced by current study and usage? To what extent is your wisdom increasing? Are you only learning from clients or are you reading magazines and books and seeking information from the internet that you can pass onto others? Incidentally, assume you are able to look at the area of your mind that contained all the information you need to justify your charge out rate. Give this area a quick check-up, is it up-to-date, in good health and in *very* regular use.

What will you be famous for?

What skills could you develop in the next year that will enable you to extend the services you provide to clients?

We have clients to serve – what do they expect? – 2nd session

Module 1
Meeting your clients face-to-face

What are clients' needs?

Suppose there were no regulatory obligations to promote demand for your services. Just for one earth shattering moment, assume the taxation authorities devised a tax system that requires no submission of financial statements with all taxes received based on some other criteria such as a triennial assessment or sales tax. And let's further assume there is no regulatory requirement to have or file audited accounts and the personal tax filing is so easy that everyone files online.

The point to consider is what the effect would be if there was no compliance work. Setting aside the impact on the number of firms and so on, one certain outcome is that you would focus 100 percent on meeting the wants of clients. There would be no compelling reason to hire an accountant and so services would be based on *want and value* as determined by the client and *not* on needs required by regulation.

Key point: Surveys inform us that the businessperson regards their **accountant as their number one business adviser** – an accolade rarely applied to the business consultant, the bank manager, the insurance adviser, members of the family or team members.

Does this accord with your own understanding of how clients view your role?

Well, it depends on which clients we're talking about. Most practitioners have higher value or *A* clients, clients, who demand your time and are happy to pay your fees. Let's assume these are business clients and about five percent of your clients.

That leaves 95 percent of your business client list. Among these there are clients who will never engage you for any service other than the most basic of compliance service. Some of them seek a *commodity service*, and most likely cost is a major factor in the decision regarding who to hire. No matter what you do to interest them in looking at planning opportunities, you know you and your firm will rarely be on their radar screen, other than when absolutely necessary.

What percentage of clients do you place in this category? Please, be careful at this juncture not to make too many assumptions and write off too many of your clients, as *Defining Edge* Practice Management Strategies is designed to challenge those assumptions! So, how many of your clients do you think would engage you for one of your other services and engage you as their number one adviser? Maybe some business owners do not take the role of adviser or facilitator seriously, but how many?

How and with who do you spend your time?

How you spend your time is a major component of your client service value equation. With 8,760 hours in a year, an owner-accountant typically spends 2,200-2,400 hours working. Of these, it is usual for between 800-1,200 hours to be chargeable. Interestingly, time recording systems do not routinely permit an analysis of the time you spend *face-to-face* with clients (*visible time*) as opposed to other time, which we call *desktop* time, or *non-visible* time.

The jaw-dropping case of the dentist's receptionist

Key point: Use this meeting as a reason to agree the date and reason for the next meeting

A clients

High net worth, best clients, niche clients, those who want to see you, those who refer you.

Your definition of A clients?

B clients

Those (typically) business clients that form the backbone of your client base.

Your definition of B clients?

C clients

Those to whom you have no commitment or real interest in seeing you in the next twelve months. They may be your 'commodity clients' or those who are looked after by managers.

Your definition of C clients?

New client meeting plan

Make available to all new clients a three stage first year meeting plan:

First meeting

The focus of this first meeting is to get to know the client and for the firm to obtain the information it requires while identifying the services and advice the client requires.

By the time you conclude the first meeting you should establish an agenda for a second meeting. The hook? Maybe looking at their accounting systems, finding out more about their business – "I'd really appreciate seeing you at your business premises." Date, time and location all agreed.

Second meeting

This meeting, wherever possible, should take place at the client's premises and probably between 2-3 months after the first meeting. Clients' offices, factories, etc, reveal so much about the client, their business, their values, their culture, and so on. This is *not* the meeting to discuss compliance matters; this is all about your client, their plans and their progress. This meeting could discuss matters such as:

- How is the business progressing compared to your expectations?
- Review the accounting records – any advice required, or affirm the client's competency in this area.
- Does the client require any advice regarding VAT or related returns?
- Are margins as expected?
- Any supplier problems, such as adequate credit terms?
- Cash flow – is there adequate working capital?
- Any trading figures available – should a flash report be prepared?
- Staffing, contractor, payroll issues?
- Feedback from customers?

And so on

Make sure they know you will write to them two months before their financial year end detailing what you need to prepare their financial statements, and that you will also meet with them around that time – the pre year meeting.

Third meeting

The pre-year-end meeting. This is the time to ensure the client knows you recognise the importance of keeping their tax liability as low as possible. As accountants, you have to work with the taxation authorities. Part of the value you offer is your firm as a highly trusted and regarded one by those bodies. Notwithstanding this, do all you can to convey to clients your commitment to ensuring their tax bill is not one penny greater than it needs to be. No one likes paying tax and one of the benefits of *having* to engage your services is your commitment hook, line and sinker to doing all you can to reduce their tax liability. Possible matters to discuss:

- Profit planning – what profit should the business report – opportunities for profit improvement?
- Capital expenditure – if any required should this before or after the year end?
- Remuneration planning
- Pension planning
- Dividend planning
- Bonuses for employees.
- What does next year's profitability look like?

This meeting also reviews the scope of records required for the completion of financial statements. Looking ahead – does the client have forecasts for the next year – working *with* the client and not just *on* the clients involves being in position as an adviser to paint the first brush strokes of the forthcoming year. Is your help required to prepare the forecasts?

A new client P.S.

Do you send out a friendly and warm email or letter before the engagement letter?

An annual meeting audit – how many meetings could you have with clients?

Client meeting calculator

Working *with* our clients not *on* them

A clients: _____

Number of times you plan to meet _____ x _____

B clients: _____

Number of times you plan to meet _____ x _____

C clients: _____

Number of times you plan to meet _____ x _____

Meeting your clients face-to-face | 2nd:1

New clients: _____

Number of times you plan to meet _____ x _____   _____

Total number of planned meetings: _____

Average meetings per month (÷12):   _____

How does this compare with meetings over the last three months:

Month _____   Meetings _____

Month _____   Meetings _____

Month _____   Meetings _____

The client meeting journey takes shape

This was the result from my own practice. After multiplying the *client numbers* by the *planned number of meetings* and adding them up, my total came to about 420 meetings. My first reaction was one of delight – after all I had earlier in the day delegated everything from my in-tray and, while there were some phone calls to return, I no longer had the work security that my in-tray provided.

I divided the total client meeting count by 12 and found the answer to be 35. That meant that I could expect to have 35 client meetings a month. With each meeting lasting about an estimated hour and a quarter that would account for 45 client hours toward my monthly target of 100 chargeable hours. But this was theory and, excellent and practical as I thought it to be, what was the reality? What next? I decided to undertake some historical research.

The story as told by my diary

As I turned the pages of my diary back to January, I counted the number of client meetings I had participated in. The highest number of meetings in one month had been 25. In January I had only met with clients on 15 occasions. Had I been on holiday? No. Except maybe I had failed to recognise the importance and needs of my clients. I had built a business that could manage clients' compliance needs but had I let my clients down when it came to being an adviser to whom they could turn?

The iceberg of time

As the captain and passengers on the Titanic found, 90 percent of the mass of an iceberg lies hidden beneath the ocean's surface. It's not visible, but that critical mass exists and supports the visible 10 percent.

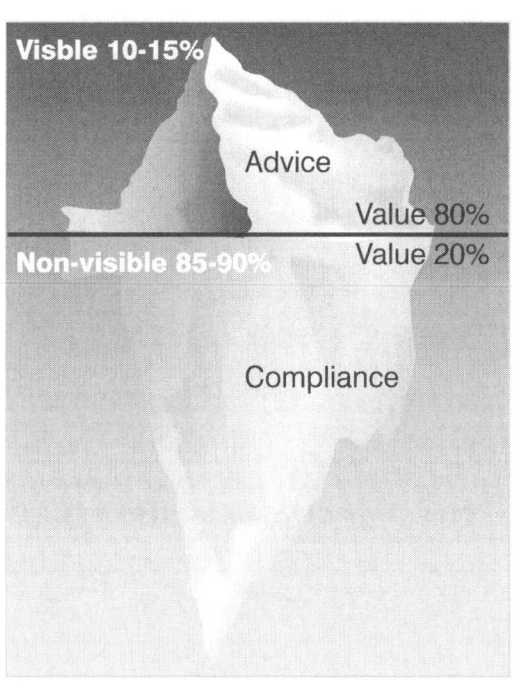

© Marrho Limited

Similarly, as accountants much of the time we spend is not visible to the client. The client knows we need their records and at some point in time their financial statements or tax returns will be completed. Based on our research we can now attach a number to those visible hours, with the typical client being face-to-face with the accountant for somewhere in the region of 150 minutes during a 12 month period.

The mass of the invisible iceberg has a major role to play to support the visible top of the iceberg. But unlike the iceberg whose mass beneath the surface is relatively constant, the iceberg's value principal serves to demonstrate the value of increasing that which is visible.

The iceberg's value principle

Key point: 80 percent of what clients value takes place in the personal interactions between the client and the partner. These are the 'magical' moments.

Question: And so, the remainder of the 80 percent of the time you spend doesn't have any value?

Answer: No, that's not what I mean. The iceberg's value principle shows us clients place a strong emphasis on the importance of the visible relationship. It's the one-on-one meetings when they hear good advice and sound judgment.

Meeting encounters uncover real needs and situations – advisory opportunities that result in defining moments that shape future client relationships
Mark Lloydbottom

The iceberg's value proposition

Key Assumption: Let's take an example whereby you spend two hours with a client over a twelve month period and then assume the value of these meetings, as perceived by the client, is 80 percent of the total service delivered. If you could increase this time from two to four hours…would the value increase to 160 percent? Considering the extra two hours might be spent on profitability enhancement, management problem solving, client centric or other future-focused services, it *should* have great value. While mathematically we should adjust the percentages so they total 100 percent, we do not suggest that the value of the invisible, compliance related work has any less value.

Key point: Thus, the iceberg of time's value proposition is that adding only three visible hours of advisory services to the client service mix potentially doubles the value to the client.

The Personal Service Gap (PSG)

Before we continue, ask yourself these questions:

Question 1: How good an accountant do you consider yourself to be?

Question 2: On a scale of 1 to 10, how good an accountant could you become?

Question 3: On average how much visible time do you spend with a typical client in a year?

Question 4: How much time do you spend discussing non-compliance matters with clients?

Key point: Giving advice about planning needs at a compliance meeting denies both you and the client the most appropriate setting for this important advice. Arrange a seperate advisory meeting to discuss planning issues.

The rear view mirror perspective

The accountants view

Our work has, for the most part, an historical perspective.

The client's view

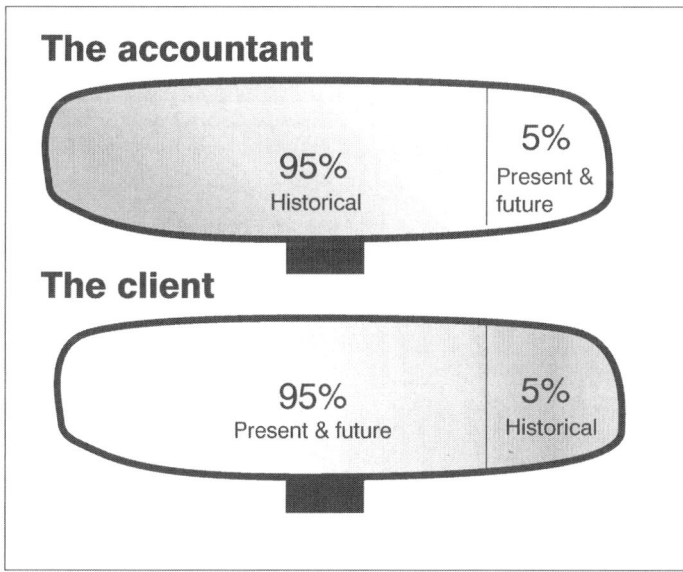

How does a business owner spend their time? Like the accountant, business owners occupy themselves with plying their trade including buying, selling, producing, marketing, managing, and making decisions. In doing so, the business owner focuses on the **present** and **future**. Yesterday is history. The hotel owner cannot sell rooms that were vacant the previous night; he or she can only sell rooms that remain unsold today. The businessperson pays heed to yesterday when paying cheques, chasing payments, dealing with service problems...and when the accountant calls.

How much time do your clients' spend on historical matters? We obviously don't know the answer precisely, but **five percent** may not be too wide of the mark.

'But my clients won't pay for the extra time' – rule of fee flexibility

Rule: Clients will pay 50 – 100 percent more than the fees they pay for compliance services so long as they can evidence the value and benefit of the additional service. Clients will pay higher prices if they receive higher value.

You manage what you monitor

How many meetings do you plan to hold with clients in the next year? How long will you be able to spend with clients? Your existing time reporting systems should be capable of being adapted to record this time separately. You might not be able to determine what time you have spent with clients in the last year, but you should be able to track this in the next year.

You may wish to evaluate the effect of this additional chargeable time and see what the likely outcome will be. When I work with firms in this area, there are usually two common outcomes:

1. The number of potential chargeable hours from owners increases, thereby increasing utilisation. The additional meetings give rise to more chargeable time without the requirement to reduce other chargeable time.

2. The commitment to visible hours increases to such an extent that the delegation of work to managers and other team members is inevitable, giving an increase in profitability.

Do you still wonder if you can charge for this time?

Yes you can. This is visible time, the client sees you face-to-face, and there is no question you are working for them. Aren't those meetings dynamic, interesting, and probing? Don't you offer solutions and bring ideas to your clients? At least with this visible time they can participate in the experience of the service, change the direction, ask questions to which they seek authoritative answers, and so on. You still have that inner self belief and confidence that it took to become an owner-accountant? Of course you can charge for your time.

2nd session

Module 2
Leveraging your client meetings

The meeting

We have looked at client needs in relation to your meetings with them. We have challenged you to look at your 'visible time' and provide a framework to focus on the potential for further client meetings. Let us restate, this is not easy; nothing worth achieving ever is. But there *is* an opportunity and a need. How many people are there that business owners, your clients, can talk to? We do not suggest that accountants are the only advisors or, on occasion, the best, but accountants are worth talking to, and our advice can be taken seriously.

One small step, not a giant leap

Our objective is *not* to lead you towards positioning yourself as a consultant. We do not suggest that these are specialist meetings or that you should necessarily look to cross-serve, (we have an aversion to the term *cross-selling*) although this may indeed result. These are 'one small step' meetings that should be regarded as an extension of the interactions you currently have with clients.

The meeting plan campaign

How do you start? Well firstly, let us agree that if one, two or even three clients say thanks, but no thanks to another meeting, that does not mean all clients will say 'no'. Those who decline probably have other matters on their mind and are not convinced about the advantage there might be in a further meeting. But, if you follow our proposed strategy, this should not happen too often, but if it does, do not be deterred, *your clients need you*!

Learn the lesson from the mime artist
– avoid the unexpected change

The mime artist employs a number of techniques to announce to the audience there is to be a change in his portrayal. The announcement is silent - it could be a 360 degree turn on stage or bringing the hand down in front of the face and so on. The mime artist makes it clear that a change 'the portrayal' is about to occur.

When you meet with clients for a compliance closure meeting you should avoid seeking to offer advice that is outside the scope of the meeting e.g. advising about other planning issues. The client is almost certainly not expecting or prepared for any serious discussion with regard to other present and future planning issues. He may need to do some research and maybe bring someone else along to the meeting – e.g. spouse. Don't catch your client by surprise or make an unexpected foray into estate planning or other non-compliance areas. Remember the lesson from the dentist's reception? Use this meeting to agree reasons for the next (planning) meeting.

Manage the client's expectations – maximise the moment

It is important to eliminate this element of surprise for a number of reasons:

- It avoids taking the client by surprise when you seek to transition the client into another service
- You need to embrace a process that allows the client to participate in discovering what planning they need to do next
- You need a process that gives the client time to think in advance so there is less on the spot thinking
- We need a process that delivers a "Yes, when can we start?"

There are a number of alternative approaches

Our experience informs us that we achieve the best results when we separate compliance work from advisory services. Thus compliance meetings, tax, audit and accounts should be the subject of one or more meetings, and advisory planning meetings of any description should be separate. Let's be clear, here I am discussing an activity that *you* engage in regularly. I recognise you have an approach to meetings, and one that works for you.

We should do *all we can to inform the client in advance* of the scope of the meeting and to give them some information they can study in advance. Clients know their business well; it is a major responsibility in their lives. When they visit you they should be familiar with the scope those discussions will encompass.

Compliance meetings

Let's take the case of the meeting to finalise the draft accounts and consider some alternative approaches:

Approach one

Some partners have the accounts in draft and a list of queries and then call the client and say, 'We have almost completed your accounts and need to meet to discuss a few points so that these can be finalised'.

Approach two – John (J – client) and Blake (B – accountant)

B. 'Good morning John, how are you?'

J. 'I'm fine, thank you.'

B. 'Good. Is now a convenient time to have a quick word regarding this year's accounts?'

J. 'Yes, by all means, I had been thinking of calling you about them. How do they look?'

B. 'Well we have taken them up to draft stage. We have one or two queries that need to be dealt with and you and I need to look through them as usual'.

J. 'Blake, when would you like to meet?'

B. 'John, here's what I suggest, I'll send you a copy of the draft accounts together with a list of the points on which we need further information. You will see that we need you to find the new vehicle finance agreement. In fact if you find this and can send it though before we meet that would be great. In any event, although the numbers in the accounts may change it will give you a chance to look at how the results are coming together. This will also enable you to assess how you feel about the year and maybe we could both discuss the performance of the business and how things are looking. When we meet I will also have had chance to look at the tax position. When are you free to meet?'

What has this approach achieved?

We have minimised the likelihood of surprises.

This scenario could be repeated for most compliance engagements – the key is to give the client as much information as possible in advance of the meeting.

Incidentally, Blake also intends to include Sarah in the meeting as she has been with the firm for three years and has been involved in the production of this year's accounts. Blake would like her to meet John, find the answers to the outstanding points, and then, hopefully, let Blake have the final accounts and tax estimates, draft letter and invoice shortly after the meeting has finished. Blake likes to post the accounts onto the clients' secure area on his website as soon as available so John can access that information.

Approach three – use an agenda

This builds on approach two, except that instead of just agreeing to send the draft accounts and points outstanding you also send an outline agenda.

Why?

The purpose of the agenda is to manage the clients' expectation regarding the scope of the meeting. As you can see from the sample agenda following, your meeting covers a range of matters that relate to your compliance work, surveys a number of current situations, and then provides an opportunity to introduce discussion on other matters. There are alternative ways to structure an agenda, but my preference is to include a circumstantial statement followed by a question. This gives the client some perspective and insight and then poses an enquiry to gain some feedback to gauge the client's perspective on the statement.

Sample meeting agenda

In attendance:

_____

_____

Year under review – compliance matters

1. Review of accounts and clearing outstanding queries

2. Review of expenditure to confirm that all expenses that can be deducted and cost allowances have been included

3. Review of our benchmark analysis and industry trends

4. Review of our tax computations, tax saving options and the due dates for payment

5. Your feedback on our services this year. 'How well have we met your expectations?'

6. Where could we improve?

Your current year – current matters

1. How is the business currently performing?

2. What challenges do you see in the future?

3. How are the results to date compared to budget?
   NB: does the client have a budget, do they need up-to-date management accounts?

4. How do you see the business developing?

5. What do your competitors do that is of interest/causing you concern?

6. Are there other points of interest that you would like to discuss relating to last year's accounts?

Personal matters – the two planning keys to life after work

1. With the increase in property values there is now a greater liability to estate taxes. Ask, 'Would you be interested in strategies to reduce your estate taxes? Or, if the client has children and has no Will 'Do you know what will happen to the children if you both die? Who will look after them?

2. We all hear about the 'Pensions Crisis' and the importance of saving for the future.

Personally, I believe that a good business owner should be financially independent of the business by the time they are 55. Have you considered what level of income you will need in retirement when the children have left, the mortgage repaid, and you have more time to pursue your other interests?'

3. Review services and charges – making sure the client is in tune with the value you have delivered

4. Discuss and agree our work this year and agree invoicing and payment terms

5. Discuss the services you wish us to provide in the forthcoming year

Other meeting questions:

1. Are there any additional services you would like to see us offer?

2. Can we help you with your business planning?

3. What else could we do to make your client experience better?

4. Are you happy with your banker and solicitor?

5. Any other matters upon that you wish to discuss?

Why do we spend so little time with clients?

- Time pressure arising from your client portfolio – Delegate some of this work
- Clients do not wish to spend time with you – Our experience is that most clients wish they could spend *more* time with their accountant
- Uncharted territory, talking to a client when *you* brought up a topic rather than responding to one *they* have raised – A professional is responsible not just for the compliance work that clients must have, but for drawing a client's attention to and suggesting solutions and give advice in additional areas that clients may not necessarily realise they need.

Question 1: On a scale of 1 to 10 how competent and confident are you when it comes to advising on matters relating to compliance matters: audit, accounts, tax and so on?

Question 2: On a scale of 1 to 10 how good are you at communicating with clients on these matters?

2nd:2 | Leveraging your client meetings

You should expect to rate yourselves highly in both these areas. You are, after all on familiar ground. This is what you are trained for, you are up-to-date and relate to this work day in, day out. You should be both confident and competent in these matters. To have *outer confidence* you must have *inner competence,* this is what clients pay for.

How much of your chargeable time relates to these matters?

Question 3: On a scale of 1 to 10 how competent and confident are you when it comes to advisory services?

Question 4: On a scale of 1 to 10 how good are you at asking questions and communicating with clients on advisory matters?

With each of these four questions ask yourself how good you would like to be. Then, consider what steps you need to take to improve your score. Then, implement!

2nd session

Module 3
And action....The client planning meeting

For the purposes of this module we assume that all matters related to compliance services are, for the time being, set to one side. We have suggested one approach of delivering non-compliance services is to arrange a separate advisory meeting with an agenda so that both parties agree in advance the scope of that meeting. That agenda might be no more than a letter or email confirming the appointment and your understanding of the purpose of that meeting.

Before the meeting, both you and your client should have the opportunity to consider the contribution of each to the meeting. What questions will you bring to the meeting? How will you open up the areas of most concern? Be sure beforehand to identify matters to be discussed. What information will you present, in what format will you present it, and what possible outcomes may ensue?

Questions are like a searchlight

There are many benefits of asking questions:

- You can confirm or correct information you have gathered from other sources
- You acquire additional information that helps you understand the client and their needs
- You may discover the new *hot buttons* for the client
- You demonstrate your expertise by the quality of the questions and your understanding of the client's situation
- Asking the right question can motivate the client to take action
- The more you ask *appropriate* questions the more successful your diagnosis of the client's needs and the better the outcome of the meeting.

You are the expert

In your role as accountant, your client engages you as an *expert* to work primarily on their *compliance* needs as one who has the in-depth knowledge and mastery of your technical skills. In your role as *expert-adviser*, you make recommendations as you help develop the solutions to client problems that relate directly to this technical work. As you *advise* in these areas you provide analysis and answers to client needs. It is when you advise in these technical areas that you put in place the cornerstone of your client relationship and build the client's trust in you.

You need to 'cross-serve' to give outstanding service

How does this create value?

Clients buy from you because they recognise they have a need and trust you to be of value to them. If you have been instructed by your client to advise, you already have evidence that the client perceives your value as an adviser.

The key is to ask good questions and then sit back and listen to the reply. A good doctor asks probing questions that develop based on patient responses and in turn the doctor reflects back insights and understanding regarding matters that affect the patient's health. A self-help group seeking to free themselves from a particular habit is often asked to look within themselves as the facilitator seeks to empower them to find and secure solutions to their own needs.

We know that value is a complex proposition, so we should not allow our objectivity or fear of diagnostic questions to stand in the way of uncovering clients' real needs.

Key point: Remember that compliance services are historically driven while your role as adviser is more focussed on the present and future. Helping clients identify options and make plans and changes to achieve personal and business goals has great value.

Are there competitors for your advisory services? Undoubtedly. But given that many advisory needs entail a significant amount of personal knowledge, there is a hurdle that clients must overcome if they want to engage another individual or firm other than one they are used to working with on their personal and business finances.

Key point: The likelihood is that if you don't give them the advice, they possibly won't receive any and will suffer from not hearing your insight and solutions.

The accountant, who already works alongside clients, is in pole position to become a *ready* and *steady* supplier of advisory and extension services. Becoming a ready supplier requires you to be focussed on providing advisory services, investing in your skills so that your expertise is duly honed. Becoming a steady supplier happens over time as you develop your client relationships and as you increasingly find yourself in the client's advisory zone.

The more your confidence grows, the more you deliver value. Clients will find you a sounding board, a fount of knowledge and inspiration and wisdom, someone they can talk to with confidence, someone who understands, inspires trust, is discerning, insightful and penetrating in their analysis.

What does the adviser role take?

You have the clients, the knowledge, and the desire. What personal skills does it take to be an adviser? The breakthrough ingredients that go into the mix of the adviser include:

Communication skills

How well do you communicate?

Empathy

How well do you understand your clients feelings?

Some specifics

Here are two examples of cornerstone planning, where the expert-adviser can position himself in the client's *advisory zone*.

For example, firstly in a meeting you may comment on the state of the stock markets, the impact of stock market downturns and the implications for investments and retirement planning. The client may respond with an observation that enables you to ask, "What would it mean to you to be more certain that you will have an adequate income in retirement?" Alternatively, you may enquire what level of income might the client need to live on in retirement if they were to retire now.

Secondly, an alternative scenario may be to ask the client if they have thought about the knock-on effect of their wealth-building success in relation to their estate planning, and what view they take of their increasing liability to estate taxes and the effect this will have in reducing the wealth that pass to their heirs. Today, our life expectancy is greater than ever before, but we live with less of an eye on the future than perhaps should be the case. We may believe we will live beyond 70, but we cannot, of course, be certain. What would you find if you spend time with clients helping them 'explore' the future, their income requirements and the adequacy or otherwise of their planning?

Client planning needs and opportunities

If you were to list five common *medium-term* planning matters for a client what might they include? First, let us work toward defining *medium-term*. *Long-term* and *short-term* are relative in just the same way as hot and cold is relative and so it is important not to focus too much on any particular period of time. Some define long-term by reference to key personal and business objectives, such as making it to retirement day fit and healthy with adequate wealth and income. Others are more short-term oriented in their perspective and cannot focus that far ahead. In that case you need to allow the client to establish the boundaries of time for planning purposes. Thus *medium-term* could be viewed as 2-5 years, or even 6-10 years. If we attempt to impose our definitions, especially any that are too far forward, a client may nod and agree, but never pursue any interest in a follow-up advisory meeting because they do not relate to our perception of priorities, time and planning. You can unlock your clients' view of the more strategic challenges by asking such questions as:

- What long-term challenges do you see on the horizon?
- Where do see yourself/your business in the future?
- What opportunities do you see in the future?
- Have you ever considered what you would do if you were not running the business?

Whatever the client's view of planning, you should learn about the client's long-term drivers. That enables you to put in context the decisions the client needs to address to achieve their long-term aspirations. It also sheds light on the extent to which current events may need the client to adjust their plans to achieve the long-term objectives.

The outcome for you from acquiring this information

Now you may have a better understanding of your client's perspectives on the future. It may be that you heard a series of vague responses but you will likely gain some important pieces of information you can fit into your client's planning jigsaw. The key objective is to talk with your client and take them on a journey to help them peer into their future. This may be the first time your client has thought through their dreams and objectives, the results from their 60,000+ hours in business. To what extent can you help them formulate the plans and actions they need to take in the next 12 months to progress their journey towards their goals and dreams. What have you learned that you can store away to enrich your future client exchanges and advisory opportunities?

Default to medium-term rather than long-term planning

There is some evidence that long-term planning does not feature very highly on the accountant's list of priorities. In fact, there is a view that long-term planning has the proverbial 'kiss of death' attached to it because we do not know what will happen next week or next month and so long-term planning is not a reality. Maybe a trip to Mars is more likely than getting committed to long-term planning. But, if we can connect clients with a relevant and current planning proposition they can relate to, they may be interested in our advisory services.

Let us explore one approach to a range of five planning needs that are common to most business owners – and others as well.

Five essential plans

1. Life plan for the year ahead (probably not a fee-earning opportunity)

This comprises plans for life as you live it on a day-to-day basis, with no overall emphasis on long-term agendas.

In my life plan I have embedded a series of sections on personal development, personal monthly finances, budgets, health, weight, exercise, travel, spiritual goals, social goals, sporting plans, family goals, cultural and entertainment goals. The key with regard to these intentions is to find purpose and direction in setting time aside to personally plan and include my family in the exercise.

Where does my zeal for planning come from? It just developed over the years as I found that it works. Probably the quote that says, 'If you don't know where you are going any route will get you there', has been a reminder of the benefit of life planning. I probably deliver each year on about 95 percent of my plans, which is why I intend to keep up my annual planning routine.

2. Business plan (fee potential)

For many years I was the managing director of both Practice Track and PracticeWEB, companies I founded that were devoted to delivering management and marketing solutions to the accounting profession. Both companies had business plans that were updated annually. Incidentally, while I was owner of those companies they both increased their turnover and profits consistently year-on-year over a 15-year period. Did my commitment to planning help? Yes. My planning time provided an essential opportunity to focus and plan strategy. In the same way as a sports coach lays out his tactics before a game, so I would prepare and review my business blueprint with all the team members, who incidentally could access the plans on the network and see the detail that lay behind the Executive Summary of Business Plans for the year.

Should you be involved with your clients and their business planning? Yes, but as with all these plans, make sure you have one first. If you do you are a wiser adviser and a more persuasive advocate of planning. I have surveyed accountants at seminars over many years and asked, 'How many of you have a written and up-to-date business plan?' The response leads me to conclude that less than half of accountants have such a plan. So if you do not have a plan, maybe you are not committed to planning?

But, *if* less than half of accounting firms do not have a plan, then maybe 50 percent or more of other businesses do not have a plan either and may not be easily persuaded to commit to a plan. Is there an alternative? Yes. Use a **key performance indicators** plan.

Key performance indicators (KPIs) (fee potential)

One approach you could adopt within your firm and recommend to clients is to use *key performance indicators* (KPIs). KPIs are quantifiable measurements, agreed to beforehand, that reflect the critical success factors of an organisation. KPIs enable a business to define and measure progress towards its goals.

KPIs will differ depending on the organisation. A business may have as one of its KPI the percentage of its income that comes from return customers. A school may focus its KPIs on graduation rates of its students. A customer service department may have a KPI of percentage of customer calls answered in the first minute. KPIs include regular reporting of such numbers as sales, production volumes, margins, number of customers, average spend per customer, visitor numbers – the key numbers that are important in the business and that inform management about business performances.

Whatever KPIs are selected, they must reflect the organisation's goals, they must be key to its success, and they must be quantifiable (measurable). The decision as to which numbers to monitor could be taken alongside you as the accountant. Accountants are after all the *masters of measurement* and should be intimately involved. The selection of KPIs is one that clients find interesting as KPIs are not limited to financial targets. For example a restaurant might focus on the number of diners in a week; a travel company might wish to focus on the number of enquiries and the conversion rate; an internet business might monitor site unique visitors and so on. Having selected the KPIs, the business requires the management information systems for gathering the data as well as a plan to either 'nudge up' the numbers or drive them down. Given that KPIs are influential numbers and their movement impacts profitability, position yourself so you can work with clients on a plan to manage their KPIs.

I once worked with an entrepreneur who suggested that you can monitor and drive any business forward by managing five carefully selected numbers. I have thought about that since and while I do not believe that five is a sacrosanct number, I have found the principle a sound one in that if you choose the most important numbers and manage them, many other areas fall into place. For example, in my accountancy business, I monitored these five numbers:

1. Monthly chargeable time
2. Total time
3. Number of meetings with clients
4. Number of meetings with advocates
5. Combined lockup in debtors and WIP.

If a client does not wish to commit to a business plan, spend time helping them develop their KPI plan, agreeing with them what they should monitor, the benefits and how this plan will be implemented and monitored.

3. Retirement plan (fee potential)

There is frequent media reference and regular communication from government about the need to save more for retirement. A review of news and financial websites confirms many countries face similar challenges for retirees with the inadequacy of their income in retirement. But in an era of high average personal debt, lower returns from investments than was the case in the second half of the 20th century, and relatively low interest and annuity rates, there is a general consensus that this is a problem that needs addressing. If we assume it is not government that will solve the problem we must assume the responsibility individually, and your role as accountant with your financial and business expertise becomes pivotal, regardless of whether or not your firm offers financial services advice.

4. Wealth plan (fee potential)

How will the client build their wealth? What will this look like? What role does investment advice and tax efficiency have to play in this? What gifts should be bestowed on family and others along the way? What is the effect of the recession?

5. Estate plan (fee potential)

Who are the heirs? How will children in a blended family be dealt with in the estate? What tax planning should be considered? What is the role of life insurance? Who will be the Executors? What are the implications of and for the business? How do charitable matters, guardians for minor children, and so on, affect the plan? What legacies should be included? What role should trusts play?

What short-term planning issues might clients have?

Before we look at these, we should examine a number of points:

First: your list of planning issues grows in proportion to your knowledge and experience. Why? Because your insight, understanding and *multi-level questions* (questions that drill down into a situation) are influenced greatly by what you know.

Second: you may consider that these issues would be more appropriate in medium or long-term planning. The key is that if your client, for whatever reason, has brought this to the top of the issue pile, this is his perception and therefore may be a good place to start.

Third: much has been written about *change management* and how to make change happen. Any change is almost invariably accompanied by some *loss*, and it is loss that leads onto grieving (there are five stages in the grieving process). Therefore, we should always approach advising clients carefully and be mindful of the fact that something almost certainly has to be lost to achieve progress. Also, with all the other activities and responsibilities going on in life, there is not always the time to make change. There is *no* gain in impressing the client with your wide range of solutions if the client does not have the *change capacity* to implement them, no matter how good they are. If the client does not make the change happen, *both you and* the *client* have a problem because advice the client has paid for has not been implemented, and so, for whatever reason, the client has not received value.

Fourth: consider the framework for the delivery of this service. Taking into account the limited change capacity we all have, you could make this service available on the basis of a regular monthly or bimonthly meeting. In this way you do not have to 'sell' the next appointment and you do not feel obliged to continually come up with new ideas.

Fifth: what is the ultimate test of a client's satisfaction with your advisory services?
- Is it their telling you they are happy with the services? No.
- Is it the client paying his or her account on time? No.
- Is it if the client recommending your services to others? No.

The litmus test of a client's satisfaction and evidence that a client has received value is when the *client comes back* for more of the same type of service.

Sixth: a word of caution. One reason why the results from advisory meetings are not as successful as they could be is that perhaps the client needs to involve others in the discussions. This is particularly true when the outcome may need to be 'adopted' by others who will be responsible for implementation or who will be impacted by the outcome.

Involving others changes the dynamics of the relationship with the client and requires personal and facilitation skills to ensure that any wider-attended meetings and discussions make the progress intended.

Areas where you can question, listen, be empathetic, and advise include:

- Personal issues and challenges
- External issues and challenges
- End results
- Business culture issues and challenges
- Business foundation issues and challenges
- Operational issues and challenges

We started our look at short-term planning by eliminating the types of work we do not consider to be advisory work. We have suggested a number of ways to perform this work including ad hoc meetings or a regular client-meeting plan. How long will this work take? That depends. The minimum length for an advisory meeting is normally about an hour. You will determine the maximum length of a meeting depending on whether it includes diagnosis, fact-finding, brainstorming, filtering of options, recommendations, and illumination and strategies culminating at some point with an agreed action plan. The action plan should include details of the actions agreed. Can an action plan be agreed? Who will do what and by when? What resources will be required? What will be the end results?

Be aware that you are unlikely to regularly meet with clients for more than four hours and retain your status as an adviser. You may in this circumstance become more akin to a consultant.

Adviser or consultant?

We have known accountants who found their path as an adviser rewarding and successful – so rewarding in terms of their personal job satisfaction that it led them to specialising and becoming a consultant. Experience and meeting with accountants who have followed this path has shown that a role as consultant can conflict with being the accountant.

Most accounting firms' structure involves having a partner as primary client manager being responsible for between 200-350 clients. Thus, for a client portfolio of, say, 250, and a chargeable hours target of 1,200, the simple average time per client is just over four hours. Now, we realise that taking an average per se means little as more time will be spent with some clients and inevitably less with others. However, we find that partners on average do not spend more than two visible hours a year with clients and between 250-350 visible hours per year in total. You can increase this by spending two more hours with 75 of your *A* and *B* clients; the additional 150 visible hours increases your total visible time as a proportion of your total client chargeable time to between 40-50 percent. That may well be a desirable and appropriate goal, but it starts to change the balance of a partner's time. If you pursue this and become too successful, you will need to hand over some of your clients to others.

We suggest that where work takes longer than four hours, and where meetings of four hours plus are increasing in number it is time to acknowledge that you and the firm are developing a consulting business. However, some firms that have committed to a consulting division have discovered that the model needed to build a successful consulting division is quite different from that required to build a successful accounting firm, and results in a new range of challenges within the firm. And so, with this word of caution, as building a consulting practice is not the focus of this programme, we move onto the revenue potential from this advisory work.

Making the commitment to invest

One of our coaching themes is that you should do more to discover your clients' needs and engage in being more of an adviser that is the case at present. If you believe that being an adviser is a role that you need to pursue, evaluate your skill set, identify your strengths and knowledge deficiencies, decide what your needs are for personal development and how you will meet them, and prepare to invest in yourself. This is an investment from which both you and your clients will see a return.

There are a range of software programs and organisations available to assist you with your compliance responsibilities. Also available are programs that may be used by the accountant in the delivery of a range of advisory services. While programs of this nature have merit, avoid seeking to shoe horn clients into a process you have bought but often do not lead to successful implementation. These programs can augment the advisory work and assist with marshalling information or situational analysis.

To qualify as an accountant probably involved between 1,500-2,500 hours of study. To maintain those skills may require between 75-150 hours study a year. How many hours will you invest in the next 12 months in advancing your skills?

The return on investing in your own skills

The **first** return will be a personal one, as you learn more about yourself and how to manage and reflect on how to apply the skills and procedures learned. As with this programme, you may find that a lot of what you learn is obvious. Accept with an open mind that you will find ways to apply what you learn. As you absorb the ideas, processes, strategies in your mind they will be easier to recall when you are with clients. If you implement what you learn you reinforce the advantage for yourself.

The **second** return comes from applying what you have learned to your friends and family, your business, and your work colleagues. I read the book by Hyler Bracey called *Managing from the Heart*. Hyler's book is less than 200 pages long and is a straightforward book with a simple but powerful message about how to improve any relationship, especially those in the workplace. Hyler uses the word *heart* as an acronym standing for:

2nd:3 | And action...the client planning meeting

Hear and understand me

Even if you disagree, don't make me wrong

Acknowledge the greatness within me

Remember to look for my loving intentions

Tell me the truth with compassion

I have learned the acronym off by heart and frequently pass it on to others. I share this with those who lean towards an autocratic style as well as those who struggle with workplace relationships.

The **third** return comes from an increase in chargeable time. By now you have probably worked out some potential new ways of spending time with clients and from this should flow increases in chargeable hours and higher value time that can be billed at premium rates. You need to live in the reality of needing to change the way you advise and to extend the visible time with clients delivering your new advisory services.

Module 4
Outstanding service –
The rewards can be substantial

Why clients change accounting firms

Service sensitivity among clients has important implications for accountants. It means that clients increasingly expect outstanding service. If you don't give it to them, someone else might be asked to act.

Most people dislike changing accountants. They have to find new accountants whom they hope will prove more competent or more personable than the previous ones; they have to answer a lot of routine questions to familiarise their new accountants with information about their financial background; and they have to face the unpleasant task of firing their old accountants whom they previously had trusted with intimate confidences. All this causes stress. An accountant has to really turn people off to lose them as clients. And yet some accountants do. Why? How?

Research studies over the last 20 years have demonstrated conclusively that customers and clients are much more likely to switch suppliers/professionals because of perceived service quality problems rather than for price concerns or product quality issues.

The evidence is clear: The reason clients change accountants is, in a word, 'service!' (or the lack thereof). What clients want and are willing to pay for is outstanding service.

Outstanding quality doesn't cost; it pays

In my experience firms the public considers 'high quality' *for whatever reason* (and it could be their size, office appearance, reputation, or whatever) can charge prices from *20 percent* to as much as *50 percent* higher than competing practices of the same size in the same market.

We conclude that, in the long run, the most important single factor affecting an accounting firm's financial performance is the *perceived* outstanding quality of its *service* (in the sense of 'the way its treats clients') and its *services* (in the sense of 'the intangible product it sells to client'), relative to those of competitors.

Note, however, that we refer to *perceived* outstanding quality, which is not the same as the typical accountant's view of quality as 'conformity to professional standards'. Our view demands an entirely new perspective – one that calls for viewing quality *externally*, from the client's perspective, rather than *internally*, from a systems-driven, quality-assurance point of view.

Making the effort to refocus your ideas about quality is clearly worthwhile. In addition to our own experiences, studies too numerous to mention show that delivering outstanding service produces measurable benefits in profits, cost savings, and market share.

We would never say that price is *un*important, but clients of all types can and do pay a premium for services and products that excel in perceived quality. Look for example, at Lexus, Coutts, Harrods and even Google who all provide outstanding quality.

Key point: Outstanding service can enable you to command higher prices.

The outstanding service quality revolution

Just because clients are becoming more demanding of outstanding service and more sophisticated about recognising it doesn't mean that all the accounting firms in the global economy are jumping on the bandwagon. Far from it. Some lead the revolution, some follow, and some sleep through it. Consider these various degrees of commitment that firms display towards service quality:

- **Going out of business.** These firms are so out of touch with their clients that they are on the way down the tubes. Some know it, some don't.
- **Plodding pursuit of the average.** These firms are probably in business to stay, but service quality is not part of their strategy.
- **Present and accounted for.** These firms know they are in the service business and instinctively respect doing at least the basics. However, most of them enjoy only a 'natural market share', which means the share of the market they are entitled to merely by virtue of showing up. Service quality doesn't play a major role in their client service proposition.
- **Making a studious effort**. These firms are on the move, and they work hard to make outstanding service their competitive weapon. Client-centredness has become a driving force for developing the firm's business culture. They are innovatively reformulating and rethinking their organisation's image and focus.
- **Service as an art form.** There are few of these in the accounting profession. For a good example, we must still look to other businesses such as Harrods, Ritz-Carlton, Lexus, or the Priory Clinic. The mission of management is to preserve and refine the firm's image of outstanding service.

As a professional, you must think about quality as more than something you do to avoid a negligence claim, or to impress your professional colleagues, or to satisfy your desire for professional challenge. You need to think about clients' needs and preferences. Quality is more than a technical problem to be solved; it is a competitive opportunity.

What is outstanding service?

What is service of *outstanding quality*? And just what does *quality* mean?

Before we answer these questions, notice that clients do not use the term *quality* in the same way that accountants do.

Example: You may remember an occasion when you delivered high quality professional work that your client neither recognised as such nor appreciated. You may have invested a lot of time and effort in handling an unforeseen contingency, perhaps in a very creative way. But because your client did not expect the contingency and was not aware of it, the client was irritated at the extra expense and delay rather than thankful for your superior professional skills!

So we must first address, 'For whom do we define *outstanding service*? Ourselves or our clients?'

The traditional view of service quality

An accountant's emphasis on quality is normally focused on the technical aspect of service delivery. We have forms, procedures and reviews all dedicated to delivering internal quality.

The client's view of outstanding service

Clients do not buy services they buy what services will do for them. Thus clients focus on how they are treated, how helpful you are and their perception of value for money.

Key point: If you want to do an outstanding job for a client, it is crucial you know what problem the client thinks you are solving.

Your 'invisible report card' from your clients

The invisible report card your clients give you reflects their judgement on your service. And those quality opinions result from comparing what they expected before receiving the service with their actual experience of the service. In other words, client satisfaction (the grade on your report card) equals client perceptions of what they received minus client expectations of what they thought they would receive. For those with an analytical mind (which includes lots of accountants), this formula expresses the concept:

$$Q = P - E$$

Where Q is outstanding service quality, P is client perceptions, and E is client expectations.

In other words, your grades on clients' mental report cards for your service equal client perceptions of what they received minus client expectations of what they thought they would receive. Nothing in the equation has anything to do with reality as seen by accountants! Client perceptions and expectations are completely subjective.

Reality is what you can perceive clearly

Use the perception principles

The key factor in client satisfaction is not how good you are at your profession, but how good your clients perceive you to be – in other words, your image. And the key factor in marketing success is not how good you are at your profession, but how good prospects and advocates perceive you to be. It's easier to create a good impression in the first place than to change a bad impression once formed.

The key factors in determining your image are summed up in the following two perception principles.

Perception principle number 1: People perceive that your performance in non-business settings reflects your performance in your profession.

Perception principle number 2: People perceive that your performance in one area of your business reflects your performance in all other areas of your business – especially the ones they cannot see.

The missing side of service quality

In professional practice, *technical* quality is created inside the firm, and the firm's personnel are usually the only people conscious of it. *Perceived* quality is the face the practice presents to the outside world.

The key to ensuring outstanding service

Looking again at the service quality equation, you see only two factors that determine client satisfaction: client expectations and client perceptions. Therefore, to improve your scores with clients, you can 1) lower client expectations, 2) raise client perceptions of what they are have actually received, or 3) do both.

The key to ensuring outstanding quality service is to meet or exceed what clients expect from you. Therefore, you must determine exactly what problem the client wants you to solve and exactly what good feelings the client seeks from you.

Even new clients with experience of other accounting firms may have strange ideas of the type of service you should render. And for new clients who have never worked with an accountant, it's even worse: Their expectations come from unconscious predictions they make about what you are likely to do. In other words, people with no prior experience of our profession are uncertain regarding what we do and what results accountants routinely achieve. Often, clients form their opinions about various professions from film and television portrayals of doctors, lawyers, and so forth. They don't know exactly what to expect, and their expectations could be way out.

Key point: Client's expectations and perceptions reflect reality the way they see it; they may not reflect reality the way you see it.

What you give a client may not be the same as what your client receives. That is, what you think you deliver and what your client perceives they get may have little relationship to each other.

Client expectations may have little relationship to reality as the accountant sees it: Clients really buy the solutions that they expect from you.

Both inexperienced and experienced clients judge service quality by weighing the difference between their expectations and their perceptions. However, for prospective clients or new clients whom you have not yet served, their expectations are only predictions that they unconsciously make about what is likely to happen when you serve them. In other words, people with little experience of you are uncertain regarding the likelihood of a favourable experience of you. They base their expectations on what they would like you to provide, not what you will or even should provide.

On the other hand, existing clients have considerable experience of you. Their expectations are what they *want* you to offer rather than what you *will* offer. Existing clients are fairly certain what to expect.

New clients with significant prior experience of other accounting firms have expectations closely resembling the expectations of existing clients. This is because they have rather definite ideas of the type of service you *should* render.

To get clients to grade your services as high quality, you must learn what clients really expect from you. This means you must ask good questions and listen – really listen – to your clients. And you must make sure your clients have realistic expectations of what you can accomplish. This requires good communication in both directions.

Key point: Clearly it is crucial with all new clients to determine why they left their previous accountant, if they had one, and what they expect of you. What, exactly, is the problem they want you to solve? Make sure you don't repeat the mistake(s) of the previous accountant.

How to turn clients into advocates

By delivering outstanding client service and being prepared to ask for new business and referrals.

Remember that: Reality is what you perceive clearly.

Quality and value – The keys to clients coming back and making recommendations – 3rd session

Module 1
Your report card – Raising the bar

As the accounting firm's first step toward managing the total client experience, you must understand the *clues* or *indicators* you are sending to your clients – the grades on your invisible, report card. 'Anything that can be perceived or sensed – or recognised by its absence' – is an experience clue.

Obviously you must help solve the client's problem as no amount of good feelings can compensate for an unsolved problem. Not so obvious is that the good-feelings indicators can work synergistically with the solutions-to-problems indicators to dramatically increase the client's perception of outstanding service.

You cannot simply state your value to clients in terms of problem-solving versus price. Instead, your value is composed of **both problem-solving and emotional benefits clients receive minus the financial and non-financial burdens they bear.**

How do clients judge your performance?

What clients perceive clearly defines their reality. The problem is that so much of what you do for them is not visible to them.

Key point: Reality is what you perceive clearly.

Clients don't see the *actual work* you do to produce the results they perceive, nor do they appreciate the technical complexity, precision, or degree of compliance this work entails. The days of continuing education you invest in your team, the quality reviews your documents or reports go through, and the investment you make in your professional library every year – all of this are invisible to them.

Most clients view what accountants do as some form of magic which I call the *black tent phenomenon*. We take their records into our *sanctum sanctorum* where mere clients are never admitted, and in that inaccessible place we perform secret rites, slay secret dragons, and chant magic incantations. Eventually, we emerge from the black tent with financial reports, tax returns, and other esoteric pieces of paper that HMRC or the bank, demand of the client.

To the client, our services can appear quite unreal. They can see what they *think* is the output, the tangible representation of the service, but your input is generally incomprehensible to them.

Even though many accountants measure quality in terms of compliance with professional standards, clients know little about such standards, and care even less. The technical aspects of your service are of little interest to most clients. Occasionally they are able to perceive the service outcome – what you accomplished – but, even then, they have little clue as to how you accomplished your results in the *black tent*.

Yet clients make decisions regarding the quality of your service every time they pay your invoice. How do they do it? If they cannot judge the technical quality of your service, what criteria do they use? Just how do they decide whether you do a good job?

Let's analyse the process by which clients grade you by mentally comparing their evaluations of what they receive with what they expected.

Generally, there are eight criteria by which clients evaluate your services. The list may be longer for some clients and shorter for others. But *generally* clients use a combination of the following criteria:

- Timeliness
- Reliability
- Competence
- Communication
- Assurance
- Tangibles
- Responsiveness
- Empathy

Remember, clients do not necessarily evaluate these in the same way as you might do. Since much of what they need to make a full evaluation is either invisible or incomprehensible to them, they use what they can see to make a judgement about what they cannot see.

It is rather like watching sparks and lava issue from the mouth of a volcano – from what you can see you infer what you can't see – a vast reservoir of molten rock beneath the surface.

The proposition here is simple: To provide outstanding service you must exceed the client's expectations, which means what they *perceive* you to be doing must impress them. So, as we review and discuss these criteria below, think about how you can *demonstrate* your capabilities in each of these areas in ways that your clients can perceive clearly.

Timeliness

Timeliness includes providing prompt service, fast turnaround, and meeting deadlines and due dates.

Questions to think about:

- What are your clients' expectations regarding your timeliness?
- How do they judge whether your delivery was timely?
- How can you improve timeliness?

Reliability

Reliability is the ability to provide the promised service dependably and accurately. It includes timeliness. The client judges you on how dependable you are. It includes keeping your commitments.

Questions to think about:

- What are your clients' expectations regarding reliability? How do they judge your reliability?
- How dependable do your clients think you are? How about others in your firm?

Competence

Competence is the client's perception of your technical ability. Competence includes performing the service correctly the first time.

Questions to think about:

- What are your clients' expectations regarding competency? How do they judge your competency?
- How dependable do your clients think you are? How about others in your firm?

Communication

Communication is how well you keep clients informed about their engagement and its outcome. It includes those aspects of client interaction where the accountant presents himself or herself as a 'great guy' or 'great lass', good adviser; knowledgeable, and so on.

Questions to think about:

- What are the client's expectations regarding communication?
- How do you know how often to talk to a client regarding an engagement in process?

Assurance

Assurance is the client's feeling that their problem is in good hands. It involves the knowledge and courtesy of your frontline and their ability to convey trust and confidence. Assurance also involves credibility, which includes trustworthiness, believability, and honesty. It means having the client's best interests at heart and demonstrating care and concern. Assurance is the reason for the old saying, 'People don't care how much you know until they know how much you care'.

Questions to think about:
- How can you improve your 'bedside manner'?
- Are there aspects related to physical and financial security that need to improve?
- How good is your firm's name and its reputation?
- How good are your frontline at generating trust and confidence?

Tangibles

Tangibles include your physical presence, evidence and souvenirs of your service, your reception and other facilities, equipment, your website and the appearance of your personnel.

Questions to think about:
- Does your personal appearance need upgrading?
- How can you improve your tangibles for your clients?
- What sort of appearance do your other client-contact people present?
- Does your website need refreshing?

Responsiveness

Responsiveness concerns your commitment to help clients and provide prompt service. Responsiveness, like reliability, also involves timeliness, accessibility, and approachability. Being responsive means:

- Clients can easily access the firm by telephone (lines are not busy), calls are answered promptly, and clients barely seldom put on 'hold'
- Clients do not have to navigate a computerised telephone 'receptionist' to get to a real person
- Appointments are easy to make and are at times clients find convenient; office hours are convenient for clients
- Waiting time in the reception area is not excessive
- Key people are not out of the office when the client needs them
- The office is conveniently located
- Clients can easily access an individual by direct line and/or email

Questions to think about:
- How long does it take a client to get an appointment with you?
- Are you as responsive as you could be to your clients?
- How can you improve your personal responsiveness?
- Are you as accessible to clients as you could be?

- How can you improve your accessibility?
- Do you return all telephone calls within 24 hours?
- How long does it take for you to respond to client emails?
- Does it take more than three rings before the phone is answered?
- If your clients are placed on hold, are you sure that any music or voice message are appropriate and not annoying?
- How many call screeners do your clients go through to reach you?
- Is your recorded message on your mobile a short and clear one?

Empathy

Empathy means you provide care and attention to clients. It goes beyond mere courtesy, although courtesy is an important part of empathy, as it is of assurance.

Questions to think about:
- What is your 'thank you quotient'?
- How do you treat the client's lower-tier employees?

How do you think you score?

On a scale of 1 to 10 with 10 outstanding, rate yourself in each of these areas according to the score you think your clients would give you:

	How good are you now?	How good would you like to be?
Timeliness		
Reliability		
Competence		
Communication		
Assurance		
Tangibles		
Responsiveness		
Empathy		

Then ask yourself, how good would you like to be? If there is improvement to be made – what can you to do to improve?

What rating do your clients give you?

Have you conducted a client survey in the last twelve months?

There are a number of reasons why professional firms don't survey clients, these include:

- No commitment to structured feedback
- Don't have the time (which really means no interest in listening to clients!)
- Carried out a survey two years ago
- Got nothing out of the last one
- We're not ready to conduct a survey.

Firms who have surveyed their clients report findings that include:

- Clients who have referrals
- Clients who are unhappy about…fees, service, staff, owners
- Clients who are interested in other services
- Clients are happy
- Clients making suggestion for improvement
- Client service as perceived by the client is not as perceived by the firm.

How do you survey clients on a routine and ongoing basis?

Listening to clients is not an option, it is mandatory. The key is how to do it effectively.

The traditional and formal approach to client surveys is to either outsource the responsibility to an agency or to mastermind this internally. Experience shows firms who do this annually tend to do this two times every three years! This approach, although having value, still leaves too long a gap between surveys. Further the survey is unlikely to coincide with the delivery of service.

There are three times and two approaches you can use to solicit this valuable feedback from clients:

Paper or card survey

1. When clients visit your office. After the receptionist has offered clients a drink, have them ask, "May I ask you to complete our brief client survey while you're waiting?" The key here is to make the survey brief.

2. When sending your clients their financial statements, send them a survey *and* a postage paid reply envelope so there is no cost to the client.

3. Similarly, when you send your clients the completed tax return enclose a client survey.

Another option includes sending surveys two and three by email.

Website survey

An increasing number of firms are using a *Clients Only* area on their website to provide clients with a means of providing feedback on service.

Ask them directly

Always be prepared to ask clients directly for their feedback, "Do you feel our services met your expectations this year?" Asking clients face-to-face isn't always easy, but it does give the client clear evidence that you care. Start your question with the following result in mind. Ask the clients questions that will enable *you* to complete the following client report card:

- On a scale of 1 to 10, how happy is our client?
- Is more *TLC* ('tender loving care' or visible partner time) required?
- Have we introduced the client to our advisory services?
- Have we asked the client for referrals?

Watch carefully for client complaints or negative feedback. Realistically, there should be at least a few. Nobody is ever perfectly satisfied, especially over an extended period of time. If you don't hear an occasional negative remark, your clients are either not being candid or you haven't made it safe for them to tell you.

Beware the principal causes of service failures

Why do accountants sometimes fail to render outstanding or even merely adequate service? What causes accountants to miss the mark occasionally and get failing grades on their invisible report cards? We have identified several causes of service failures:

- Production and consumption of services partially overlap and occur simultaneously. There are inescapable interactions between frontline personnel and clients
- Not delivering value for money
- Inadequate service to 'internal customers' – other people in the firm
- Communication shortfalls
- Clients have unrealistic expectations of the service outcomes
- Viewing clients as 'cases' rather than people – seeing them impersonally
- Inadequate investment in technology, client interface systems *and* training
- Getting in 'over your head'.

How many of your service failures can be traced to one or more of these causes?

Communication shortfalls

Several types of problems occur:

1. The firm overpromises

2. The firm fails to stay in touch; or

3. The client misunderstands the accountant's communication.

The client may feel, 'they can't be trusted or relied on', 'I got no response', or 'my accountant doesn't listen to me. My instructions were not followed'.

Failing to stay in touch with clients

A disproportionate number of service failures arise from accountants' failure to stay in touch with clients until a problem is resolved.

This sort of thing happens all the time – to the accountant. They are routine – to the accountant. But these are events of earthshaking importance to the client! Receipt of any notice from a taxing authority strikes fear and terror in the hearts of some clients. They may act pretty calm about it, but their guts are turning over until they get the 'all clear' from the expert. To them, these are crises comparable only to the transmission falling out of their car in the middle of a motorway at 100 miles per hour! To the accountant, it's just a routine matter.

3rd session

Module 2
Managing your moments of truth

Definition: A moment of truth: any event in which a person encounters an aspect of your firm and forms an impression of the quality of your service

Managing those moments of truth to enhance the client relationship is the foundation of building and enhancing your intangible asset – your goodwill bank. This is more important than the management of your tangible assets. Managing moments of truth may not be easy, which is why you must work on it diligently. You should regularly ask, 'How am I doing with this client? Is the relationship improving or declining? Am I keeping my promises? Am I neglecting anything?

The problem and challenge is that many moments of truth take place far beyond the immediate control of the partners. Because partners cannot be there to influence the quality of so many moments of truth, they must manage them indirectly through team members by creating a client-centred culture and work environment that reinforces the value of putting the client first.

The ten commandments of good business

These offer some pretty good advice for professionals to follow. And the best ones do.

1. Clients are the most important people in any business – in person, by mail, by email or by telephone

2. Clients are not dependent on us; we are dependent on them

3. Clients are not an interruption of our work; they are the purpose of it

4. Clients do us a favour when they call; we are not doing them a favour by serving them

5. Clients are a part of our business, not outsiders

6. Clients are not cold statistics; they are flesh-and-blood human beings with feelings and emotions like our own

7. Clients are not people to argue or match wits with. Nobody ever won an argument with a client

8. Clients are people who bring us their wants; it is our job to fill those wants profitably to them and to us

9. Clients are the lifeblood of this and every business

10. Clients are deserving of the most courteous and attentive treatment we can give them.

Module 3
Enhancing the value of what you deliver

Because your clients buy solutions to problems (and not professional services *per se*), you must discover just exactly what problem the client wants you to solve. In addition, because clients also buy good feelings, you must be concerned with the manner in which your service is delivered.

Find out what your clients need and want

Clients are like a bird in the hand: grasp them too tightly and you will crush them; grasp them too loosely and they will fly away.
David W. Cottle

You must consider two aspects of each client's needs: service outcome and operating style. Too often, accountants concentrate on providing what they think are their clients' desired service outcomes and neglect their clients' operating style expectations.

Service outcomes are the solutions the clients want – what they are trying to accomplish. Clients use service outcomes to judge the quality of your efforts. Therefore you must learn how clients will decide whether you have achieved their desired results.

Operating style refers to the manner of delivery – how your clients expect you to work. Operating style includes many client-interaction factors: How closely do they want you to confer with them? Can you upgrade them from your compliance services to your advisory services? How much do they want to know? Will they give you permission to advise, and in which areas?

Different clients need different degrees of communication, empathy, and assurance. Some clients want lots of hand holding, while others need almost none, being content for you to restrict your service to the routine of the compliance. You need to know where in the hand holding spectrum their wants, expectations, and needs are. Some very self-reliant clients want you to give them all the facts, lay out all the options, and let them decide. Some want all of these, and, in addition, they want your recommendation, which they may or may not action. Other clients want you to tell them just enough so they feel comfortable that you know what you're talking about. Then they want your recommendation, which they will almost always take.

Key point: The first rule for happy clients: Give them what they want.

Q: How do you find out what they want? A: Ask the right questions.

You can't help your clients if you don't know what service outcomes they want. To oversimplify: You should ask each client, 'What is your situation now?' and 'What would you like it to be?' This is the essence of finding out the client's problem. In practice, it's not quite as easy as that because clients often don't know how to describe their current situation in meaningful terms. Also, they don't necessarily know what is doable in the professional realm.

Because all professional engagements require cooperative effort between your firm and your client, the client has to do some of the work. Sometimes the client's only work is to give you basic information at the initial meeting, after which you're on your own. Sometimes, however, the client actively participates at every step of the process, such as in creating a personal financial plan. Sometimes, you can use the client's input to lower your fees, such as in providing year end information on accruals, prepayments, receivables and payables reconciliations and gathering any required data from third parties or organising any other information. Find out how much cooperation you can expect from the client.

Naturally, tradeoffs are involved for both you and the client. Some clients with large staffs may want to do as much of the work as possible.

Key point: In planning each service or project with a client, obtain a clear mutual understanding with the client of your responsibilities, the client's role and the required outcome.

Your goal is to have a complete mental grasp of the client's circumstances, thoughts, feelings, hopes, and concerns about this situation so that you can act in the client's best interests and stay within any agreed cost parameters. One of the key techniques both in understanding the individual client and in communicating in general is the ability to listen to the client. Good listening is more than just staying awake.

Coaching tips: to improve listening:
- Look at clients when they talk to you and when you talk to them
- Sit up straight and be alert
- Let clients complete what they are saying
- Give nonverbal feedback by nodding or smiling when appropriate
- Confirm your understanding of what the client has said by paraphrasing it back to them.

How to manage client expectations

Clients actually buy expectations of benefits that you promise them, or that they think you promised them. When it takes a long time to fulfil the promise, or if fulfilment becomes a long-term process, client anxieties can build.

Several things can increase clients' anxiety:
- If a client suspects you do not completely understand their requirements they may think you are wasting their time and money. Be sure clients feel you completely understand their requirements
- The more complex the service you perform, the less they understand what you are

doing and why. Mysteries always seem threatening to people; they feel better when they know what is going on. Always tell clients what you are doing and what you are going to do next

- The more operating procedures, management routines, and service activities they must participate in, the more likely they will feel frustrated. Even though the engagement is a duet between your firm and the client, try to minimise the amount of work the client must do

- If the service takes longer than they expected, they may become uncertain about the final outcome. Keep the client up-to-date on your expected schedule and any changes in circumstances, likely outcome or due dates

- The more personnel they must interact with, the lower their satisfaction. Keep your engagement team to a minimum size consistent with timely service.

Here are six steps you can take to exert a little more influence over clients' expectations:

1. Avoid the temptation to over-promise

2. Learn to identify extremist clients

3. Do not oversell the service outcome

4. Introduce the client to the idea that a number of factors could influence the outcome

5. Educate the client about the ongoing service

6. Stay in touch with the client throughout the service process.

Manage the tangibles

Managing the tangibles is closely related to managing client expectations. Managing expectations increases the chances of the client having realistic expectations before you render the service, whereas 'managing the tangibles' is concerned with shaping client opinions during and after you render the service.

Give your souvenirs a make-over

Souvenirs are the documents you give clients that remind them of the services you provide. How do your souvenirs differ from your competitors? Accounting software automatically provides financial statements in a standard format. As a result most firms' financial statements have common characteristics in terms of format and style. While accounting standards continue to evolve, the appearance and content of financial statements has generally not. Financial statements include a summary of income and expenditure and a balance sheet with accompanying notes to amplify and explain the numbers.

Clients collect your souvenirs

Because clients cannot hold your services in their hands like they can a widget, they often pay special attention to the souvenirs as clues to your service quality. Your souvenirs include reports, financial statements, documents, tax returns and engagement letters. To clients, the quality of the souvenir signals the quality of the service.

Your clients may pay thousands for your services, and often all they have to show for it is a few pieces of paper containing your report. Accountants frequently charge large fees for rendering opinions of various types. The value is in the opinion, not the physical report, but the physical report is the souvenir. In the case of the financial statements it records in one format the success of their business, including a comparison with the previous year. Your clients pay their hard-earned money for your service. Make sure your report shows off its value. Use heavy paper covers if you have the document bound. Consider having your firm's logo *embossed* (raised stamping in the paper without ink) on the cover page, or have your firm's name printed in the centre at the bottom. Your graphic designer can show you samples.

Your financial statements can highlight your UAP

Anecdotal evidence tells us that clients take only about two minutes to review their financial statements when the accountant is not present. You don't believe that? Most clients are now able to access financial summaries from their accounting records, while most accounting software programs include a profit and loss account and balance sheet reporting facility. The information you compile is historical and often months old, while the client is now focussed on the current month and year.

Use the financial statements to take yourself into the client's present and future

Provide your clients with *expanded* financial statements, including:

- A copy of the letter that you send clients with the financial statements. This letter includes your commentary on the client's year and the client often files this separately from the accounts. This letter is valuable for others, such as bankers, who can evidence the quality of your written advice.

- Not every client relates to their business' financial performance as shown in the accounts. Maybe they don't find it easy to relate to the way numbers are presented.

- Some firms include pie charts, bar charts and other graphic images such as histograms. These enable clients to better relate to their business' financial performance.

- The financial statements could include a summary of business trends analysis over a given time period, say three to five years. This enables clients to take a view of the key trends and direction of the financial performance over a longer time period.

- Include a one page local economic report that details insights into the local economy, key business announcements, trends in growth rates, changes in population and other information that sets clients business activities in context of the local marketplace.

Include a forecast page with three columns:

1. Last year's profit and loss account;

2. Next year's with all the numbers, where appropriate, increased by the rate of inflation, or 4 or 5 percent;

3. A column for you and your client to complete (in a meeting) based on information discussions with your client on how he or she views the outcome of the year. If the client doesn't have a budget – he or she does now!

Other reports such as:

- A business health check
- Ten ways to increase business profitability
- Ten technology pitfalls to avoid
- Ten ways to win new business
- The keys to developing a marketing campaign
- Ten reasons to visit our website
- Ten great management ideas, and
- A menu of ten services that you offer that clients find most useful.

This last suggestion is important. If you were to interview businesspeople and ask, 'What services does your accountant offer?' you would find that up to 80 percent of those interviewed list no more than three services, including tax/tax returns, accounts/audits and maybe one other.

Most clients don't know the full range of services you can provide. You could include a 'service-menu' in reception as well as on your website. When clients have a need, they will then recall the wide range of services you have to offer.

Draft accounts presentation

We refer earlier to the fact that clients do not spend more than two minutes looking at the final financial statements. In fact clients are likely to spend more time studying the *draft* accounts. These accounts are the first opportunity they have to study the *official* summary of their year. As they pore over these statements they know there are still some adjustments and the forthcoming meeting with you will delve deeper and maybe change some of those numbers.

Clients spend more time reading draft accounts than final accounts. Yet, this important report is often presented on low cost, low quality copy paper, without a bound cover.

Coaching tip – Provide outstanding service from beginning to end. Present draft accounts *and* a selection of the above reports when sending or presenting accounts to clients.

Now you have financial statements that demonstrate components of your UAP. Any other professional who sees these client financials will see that uniqueness of your service. You distinguish your firm's services in the minds of other professionals who are, or may become, your advocates.

Your tax return service

Similarly you should present tax return drafts and final versions in a high quality format. The tax return can be presented in a report format that includes, some or all of the following:

- Your letter
- Tax return

Other reports such as:

- Strategies to reduce your tax liability
- Do your estate plans need an update?
- Is your Will up-to-date?
- Plan to reduce your estate taxes
- Making your saving plans tax-efficient.

Formats for delivery of these souvenirs

While a printed format remains the most commonly used format, technology makes other formats as acceptable, if not more so. Plan to make souvenirs where requested available to clients in the following formats:

- In a secure document exchange area
- By email – but *only* through a secure server
- On CD – complete with a high quality presentation and packaging
- On a flash drive/memory stick

The job is not finished until the records are returned

When you use the laundry service in a quality hotel, you expect to receive your clean laundry, neatly pressed and presented in a cellophane cleaner bag. In some five star hotels there are sometimes notes from the cleaning department and a more elaborate style of clothes bag. In other words the clothes are returned in a better state then when they were collected from the room.

When clients receive their records back from you, they probably have no immediate need to access those records. However they are not going to dispose of them. Here is an

3rd:3 | Enhancing the value of what you deliver

opportunity to return the records in a better state than which you received them.

Some firms return records in the box or bag they came in, some in plastic bags, others in cardboard boxes. Some firms don't seem to return records at all while others even charge clients for storing their books and records!

An outstanding service approach includes being able to return records in a better state than you received them. Some firms have a selection of different sized cardboard boxes overprinted with their firm name. Select a white carton as this enables the firm's branding to appear clearly on the client's storage shelf. When you finish with your client's records, make it *your* responsibility to return their records. Charging clients for keeping records that you should return is irritating to clients and is *not* a demonstration of outstanding client service.

Module 4
Projecting a high quality image

Perception principles

In session 2, module 4 we introduced two perception principles. In this module we elaborate on them, but first let's just recap on what was said previously.

The key factor in client satisfaction is not how good you are at your profession, but how good your clients perceive you to be – in other words, your image. And the key factor in marketing success is not how good you are at your profession, but how good prospects and advocates perceive you to be. It's easier to create a good impression in the first place than to change a bad impression once formed.

The key factors in determining your image are summed up in the following perception principles.

Perception principle number 1: People perceive that your performance in non-business settings reflects your performance in your profession.

In other words, if you cheat on the golf course, your golf partners may suspect that you approach your professional responsibilities the same way. People see your performance as a tennis player, parent, coach, etc. as representative of your performance as a professional. They may not know how you handle yourself under pressure professionally, but they can tell how you handle yourself in the last 15 minutes of a school football game when your child's team is down one goal.

Perception principle number 2: People perceive that your performance in one area of your business reflects your performance in all other areas of your business – especially the ones they cannot see.

This principle works for firms as well as for individuals. People may not know how well you do research, but they can clearly perceive whether you keep your library tidy. They may not know whether you keep up with the latest developments in your specialty, but they do know whether your receptionist can pronounce their name. They may not know how well you performed the service, but they know what your souvenirs look like.

Perception principle number 3: Other people perceive a person or firm differently from the way the person or firm perceives itself.

Perception principle number 4: Other people perceive a person or firm differently from the way the person or firm *think* it is perceived.

Perception principle number 5: Different people and groups perceive the person or firm differently from one another. Obviously, your image is not the real you. In fact, you or your firm could have an image that does not represent the real you nor the calibre of service you render. In other words, your image might have as much relationship to your reality as television news does to the real world.

When someone looks at you, what do they see? You might think they see you, but actually only about 5 percent of what they see is you; the rest is your appearance, including your clothes and hairstyle! The overall effect of what they see creates a mental picture or conception that gives some clues as to what sort of professional you might be. For those who don't know you, that image, and what you might say to them, is all the information they have with which to judge you. To them, that image is the real you.

Your personal image

Your image has two parts: Your personal image and the image of your firm. Personal impressions are composed largely of appearance, communication, and actions.

1. Appearance

Appearance is just that – what you look like.

Appearance includes your clothes, grooming, posture, and gestures. People get one message if you wear business attire and a different one if you wear sports clothes. Your business suit, your tie or scarf, and your shirt or blouse give visible clues as to who you are. These say, among other things, 'This person looks like they mean business,' or 'This person is untidy'.

How would people react if you were otherwise dressed for business, but you wore trainers? Like the tough-looking movie cowboy who enters the saloon and orders milk, you would give conflicting messages that confuse others. To avoid confusing your clients or sending mixed messages, dress consistently. Generally, dress more rather than less conservatively, look richer rather than poorer, and understate rather than overstate. Create a commanding, confident image with consistent messages.

Yes, appearances can be deceiving and you can't tell a book by its cover. Nonetheless, book publishers spend millions on research each year to discover which types of cover will help sell their books.

Example: Did you ever notice a bookstore display of the same book in which half had red covers and half blue covers? Everything else was identical except the colours. Or perhaps the colours were the same but the typeface in which the book title was different. That was a market test – the publisher was testing to discover the difference colour or type style would have on sales.

These savvy businesspeople realise – for good or bad, rightly or wrongly – the cover has an influence on selling the book.

Similarly, your personal appearance sends definite messages – messages that sometimes neither the sender nor the receiver are aware of. Whether you like it or not, your appearance influences people.

Which way do you want it to influence them? Remember, 95 percent of what people see of you is only your clothes and your hairstyle.

The same applies to everyone in your firm. Every employee should project a high-quality image because the combined image created by your firm's personnel signals to the public what sort of firm you are. If people ever get to know you or your firm, they certainly have a more accurate picture of you both professionally and personally. If you do not make the right first impression, you may never get the chance to make a second impression and cultivate a relationship with that person as a client.

In other words, unless you develop a positive, professional image of yourself and your firm in the minds of clients, potential clients, and advocates, you will probably not receive those referrals, nor your clients recommend you to others.

When asked to recommend a firm, what image first comes to clients' and prospects' minds when your name is mentioned?

Many more people know *of* you than are personally acquainted with you. And many more people are only acquainted with you than really know you. The funny thing is all those people – regardless of how well they know you – have an image of you. It is the mental picture they get when your name is mentioned. The better they know you, the more accurate their mental picture.

But the converse is also true. The less they know you, the less real, first-hand information they have on what kind of person you are, and what kind of firm you represent.

Well, then, how do people form their mental picture? What information goes into their minds to make up the picture?

Questions to think about:

- What kind of message does your clothing send?
- What message does your hairstyle send?
- What do they say about you?

2. Communication

Communicate in ways that reinforce your image of high quality, including your voice, the words you use, the jokes you tell and the subjects you discuss.

Communication overlaps with appearance to include your body language, the way you walk and carry yourself, and the gestures you use. Do you stand and walk confidently, taking up a lot of space? Or do you creep into a room as though you hope nobody notices you? When you open your mouth, what comes out?

People's number-one fear – for some even more feared than death – is the fear of speaking before a group. Even if you never make a speech, the way you speak one-on-one or in social groups profoundly affects your image. Effective speaking does not automatically set you apart from the crowd, but ineffective speaking guarantees that you remain anonymous – or notorious. An offensive word, a poor choice of words, or an angry word, once spoken are irrevocable. Avoid the boring tone, the unpleasant voice, and the unpleasant personal mannerism.

You can find numerous CD and DVD programmes to help you improve your ability to speak in public. And, if you think you don't speak in public, think again. You certainly do not speak in private. Any time you talk to someone other than yourself, you speak in public. Buy one of these programmes and listen to it several times and practise, practise, practise. It will help you communicate a higher-quality, more confident image.

Do not use profanity, even if you hear the other person use it. Why take a chance on offending someone else within earshot? Also, it hurts your professional image, even to someone who is personally profane.

Humour (such as teasing or jokes) also can be dangerous unless you are good at it. Avoid long stories or jokes in poor taste (e.g. morbid, religious, ethnic, or vulgar jokes). Also, sarcasm can turn people off quickly; especially people who do not know you well.

3. Actions

Actions can speak louder than words. Actions demonstrate competence and the quality of your service far better than words. Actions include personal, business, community, and charitable activities, as well as the professional experiences people have with you.

Apply the perception principles to your discretionary, non-professional activities. To be perceived favourably by others, follow these guidelines in your leisure activities:

i. Be active

Select a project or organisation you enjoy regardless of whether or not it helps your business. It gives you a good feeling about how you spend your discretionary time. This in turn makes it easier to stay active. You can find constructive activities in community, social and charitable organisations. Community and charitable activities, such as schools and religious organisations have an added advantage that social clubs do not: Bonding occurs when dedicated people work together towards a worthwhile common goal.

ii. Be effective

Clearly, you should get involved only where you can be effective. Don't bite off more than you can chew, and avoid activities in which you cannot competently follow through on your tasks. Remember, the way you perform here indicates to others how well you perform as a professional.

iii. Be visible

Your involvement and activism demonstrates leadership qualities only if people can see you. So pick your spot with care. You can burn the midnight oil as treasurer of the Theatre Board, but you won't get as much visibility as the fund-raising chair. At the local art festival you can squirt mustard at the Lions hot-dog stand until your hands cramp up and your feet cry for help, but people won't notice you as much as they notice the membership chair.

One other thing, sow your seeds in *fertile ground* – any area that could lead to business opportunities later on. The point of your action is to expend your efforts where you can make contacts and develop relationships with the largest number of prospective clients and referral sources. In other words, 'Hunt where the ducks are!'

Your firm image

Clients' and prospects' impressions of a firm are composed of the following:

- Combined impressions of the firm's personnel, particularly the frontline personnel
- The appearance of websites, emails, documents, reports, correspondence, newsletters, and other visible products the client receives from the firm
- Office facilities, particularly your reception, client meeting rooms and equipment.

Your personnel

Have your receptionist offer every visitor some refreshment. Even if you come to collect the visitor immediately, the offer shows good manners. Visitors may carry briefcases or coats. Your receptionist should offer to hang coats on your coat rack. Visitors will want to retain briefcases.

If visitors have not finished their refreshments when you arrive, you (or maybe the receptionist) should *volunteer* to take either the refreshments or the briefcase, or both to your office or conference room.

Meet each visitor personally in the reception area; do not send a secretary to fetch them. If your visitor will be seeing more than one person in your office, each person should personally take the visitor to the next person and make the introduction.

Key point: After the welcoming appearance of your reception area, the next most powerful image of your firm prospects see is how they are greeted and treated when they enter your offices.

Your office

What sort of image does your office project? Consider the images of your office that a client or prospect sees. Close your eyes if you wish.

- Start with the view from the street. Your office building should present an image consistent with the way you want to be perceived.

Projecting a high quality image

- Your parking area can be convenient and inviting, or it can be awkward, or inconvenient. It should be well lit to contribute to a feeling of security, and it should be tidy and weed free.

- What is the first thing a prospective client sees when entering your office building? There might be something you can do to improve your building lobby/reception, even if you are only a tenant. Why not ask the landlord? The worst the landlord can do is say 'No'.

- Don't forget the view prospects see if they enter from the rear of the building.

- Your listing on the building directory should compare favourably with other companies in the building. List all the qualified professionals in your firm on the building directory or in your reception, as well as any department heads, such as firm administrator, IT manager, etc. The longer your listing, the better.

- Pay attention to what clients see when they walk down the hallway to your office entrance. These images should compare favourably with those of other professional firms.

- Prospects entering your reception area should be pleasantly surprised and favourably impressed. Your reception furniture gives prospects their most powerful initial impressions. Is your reception area conservative, progressive, expensive, cheap, first class, or 'I decorated it myself'?

- The works of art on your walls should be consistent with one another and with your firm's image, as well as in good taste. If possible, feature original art of local artists or local scenes.

- Picture your own office equipment and furniture in your mind as if you were a client.

- Imagine your office as if you were seeing it for the first time. Do you like what you see? Does it present an appropriate image to your clients? What changes, if any, should you make?

- Your car presents an image of success. Ensure it is clean and polished.

- The magazines in your reception area can demonstrate a concern for your clients' interests. Your professional journals are okay, but they shouldn't be the only thing for clients to read.

- By paying proper attention to the many facets of your image, you can send positive messages to your clients and prospects.

Your ambassadors

You have many *ambassadors* that represent your firm when you are not there. We are not just talking about the other people in your firm. Your website, client newsletters, brochures, announcements, business cards, faxes, and so forth are ambassadors that represent you when you are not around. If you think about it, that's why they are there, isn't it? They represent your firm when you are not present and keep reminding people how you are available to serve them.

Your client newsletter and eshots should project the right image. Spend what it takes to get it professionally done with high impact, relevant, quality articles that are easy to read and inform the reader about important changes as well as areas where your firm provides professional service. That is preferable to writing long, technically correct, scholarly pieces that no one but another accountant would understand.

The same principles apply to your website, brochures, proposals, announcements, and any other tangible products you provide to your clients or referral sources. What impressions do they leave with the reader?

Because prospects have few ways to judge your technical quality, they may rely on the advocacy of others when choosing a new accounting firm. Prospects will often visit websites of other firms and select a small number to interview or request proposals from before selecting a new firm. The problem is they really can't be certain what they're doing when they pick 'the best qualified' firm.

So they use any available means to reduce the bewildering number of alternatives and make their choice easier. That's why they visit websites, read brochures, and ask for written proposals.

Questions to think about:

- What do your business cards and stationery say about you? Are they distinctive or do they look like everyone else's?
- What does your website say about you?
- How do you visually present reports and documents? Does your report show its value? Your clients pay good money for your services. Mostly, those services are intangible. The only physical evidence of the service is the written report.
- Where do you produce your client newsletter? What sort image does it project?
- Who writes your proposals, and how much care do the writers devote to them?

The billing canvas – setting the scene
– 4th session

Module 1
Billing – An introduction

Perception principles

A group of accounting firms invited me to speak again at their annual conference. Prior to the start of the conference, the conference chairperson asked me, "What do you consider the number one problem facing accounting firms today?"

Wow! Tough question. Accounting firms face lots of problems. Some problems today are not the problems you faced a generation ago; some are. As the economy and the market change, so, too, do your challenges. Technology changes economies change, competition changes, laws and procedures change, accounting standards change, tax law and filing requirements change. All these change with the times. So I had to think for some time to answer that question. Then I realised that the people problems seem to remain the same year after year – owner profit share, recruitment, client relations, marketing, and so forth – because *people don't change*. So the answer that I gave her years ago still is true today. And I think it will be true for many, many years.

Pricing your services and invoicing for them is one of the most important skills in a successful practice of accountancy. However, formal university education almost never covers it; employee training seldom includes it; and even owners of the same firm rarely discuss pricing in an organised manner.

Apparently you should be born knowing how to set prices, negotiate prices and submit invoices – or else learn by osmosis:

However, pricing and invoicing are like accounting or riding a bicycle: they are skills that one must learn. As a result, the skill levels manifested by owners, even in the same firm, often vary widely. Two owners in the same office with approximately the same experience, who handle the same types of clients, and do similar work often yield strikingly different results in invoicing clients.

The income you enjoy today and the kind of lifestyle you have when you retire depend on how well you manage your firm. *Defining Edge* Practice Management Strategies will help you in this crucial management area.

Key point: The number one problem facing accounting firms yesterday, today, and tomorrow is *attitude*.

Too many accountants have the wrong attitude about certain things:
- They act as though anything less than outstanding client service is acceptable – you need your clients more than they need you.

Billing – an introduction

- They have the attitude that they don't deserve to make a lot of money.
- They feel like they have to justify everything they do.
- They have the attitude that something has to come hard to be worth anything.
- They think they have to work 50 or more hours a week to be successful.
- They feel there is something immoral about charging more than their standard charge out rates.

Here's the bad news – *As long as you have those attitudes you will not be as financial successful as you deserve.*

Here's the good news – *You can change your attitude.* It's as simple – and as hard – as changing your mind. But changing your mind requires you to form new habits. Someone once said, "Bad habits are easy to form and hard to live with. Good habits are hard to form and easy to live with."

I sometimes think the most important thing I do for some clients is to get them to rethink the way they see themselves and their relationships with their clients.

These modules are intended to help you adjust your attitude.

Here are the actual results of using some of the ideas we will discuss today:

- One firm in Birmingham raised charge out rates 35 percent with less than 5 percent client losses.
- One firm in the north of England, increase of £10,000 of net income per partner from one idea.
- Another firm, increase in revenue and profits of £100,000 from one idea.
- One firm in the south of England, increase in realisation of 7 percent.
- A firm in the north-east of England increased charge out rates 30 percent with less than 2 percent client losses.

Differences in financial performance are caused by differences in management performance.

Three top reasons accountants do not earn enough

1. Disregarding what any of your fellow owners' charge out rates may be, could you personally invoice and collect £10 per hour more for your own time?

2. If I asked all professionals in your firm "What percent of the work you do could be done by someone with a lower charge out rate, if you were better organised and if you had trained assistants available?," what would the average answer be?

3. We do not manage our firms like businesses.

Module 2
Billing myths – Surely they can't be true

Unconsciously, most accountants accept certain myths as if they were the Ten Commandments. I do not know if these myths were ever true, but they are not true today. How many of these do *you* unconsciously accept?

Myth 1: The only ethical way to price your services is by the hour. That's fair to the client and fair to the accountant.

Reality: Institutes have no ethical restrictions that prevent an accountant from pricing services on a different basis.

Independence and objectivity are essentials in accounting. Certain pricing methods, such as commissions, contingent prices, success prices, and the like, are often acceptable if the client is aware of the pricing before you start the engagement, and the pricing arrangement complies with the rules of conduct of your Institute.

Myth 2: Accountants should do the job first and think about fees later.

Reality: There is always time to discuss prices.

You must make a profit to stay in business.

Key point: Most accountants don't always accommodate to the reality that their only resources are time and expertise, and any time they give away they reduce their financial success and send the wrong message to clients.

Myth 3: Most write downs are caused by inexperienced or inefficient employees.

Reality: When the job has run over budget three years in a row, maybe it is time to rethink the pricing.

Myth 4: All clients are very price-conscious and think your fees are too high.

Some clients, not all.

Reality: Most clients give their accountant's invoice about as much attention as they give their electricity bill.

When I was a teenager, I was very concerned about what my peers thought of me. If you have teenagers, you may recognise this characteristic. I had to wear the right clothes and the right hairstyle. I had to listen to the right radio station and dance the right dances. My mother used to bring me down to earth by saying, "Son, you wouldn't worry so much what other people thought about you if you knew how seldom they did."

By the same token, I say to accountants, "You wouldn't worry so much about what clients think about your prices if you knew how seldom they did."

After 15 years of practicing accounting followed by more than 20 years as a consultant to the profession, I have concluded that accountants are more price conscious than their clients! And the clients who are most price sensitive are frequently your least desirable clients – the ones an accountant would be better off without.

Myth 5: Accountants should raise prices only when demand exceeds supply.

Reality: If accountants work smart, demand should never exceed supply.

No accountant should want to be booked every available hour because the result is the following:

- No time to plan and manage
- No opportunity to take advantage of marketing opportunities
- No opportunity to respond to client or firm matters
- No personal life.

As your firm develops, you should make more and work less, because your skills and reputation make you more valuable to clients.

Practical tips: Increase your prices – that is, the amount you charge for the value you deliver – as that value increases.

Myth 6: Further, if you raised fees, many clients would leave.

Reality: If accountants raise prices, some clients might leave, but far fewer than anticipated.

We have coached many accountants through price increases ranging from 10 percent to 35 percent. Clients notice only when the increases approach 15 percent or more

Myth 7: Alternatively, If you do good work, your client will appreciate the quality and will pay for it.

Reality: Technical quality is invisible to clients. They take it for granted.

Most clients assume, rightly or wrongly, that all accounting firms of a given size are comparable in technical proficiency. For the most part, they are right – thanks to good education and self-regulation by the profession.

Consequently, you cannot market your services by saying, "Use us! Our accounting standards are more generally accepted than those of our competitors!" (By the way, avoid the word *competitors*, especially when talking to clients, prospects, and referral sources. It is much better to call them *colleagues*.)

Myth 8: If you do not charge a client for all the work you did, they will be more likely to pay the invoice.

Reality: Clients do not know how much work their accountants do, nor how much their accountants write off.

The "iceberg of time": Clients do not know how much work you did, or how much you wrote off. If you do not value your time or your work, neither will your client.

Myth 9: If you give someone a discount on your price, they will be so happy they will recommend you to their friends or do other nice things for you.

Reality: Many accountants give new (and old) clients a discount even though the clients neither ask for it nor expect it.

Think about this: Starting a new client off at a reduced fee teaches them to expect first class service for an economy price. This makes it hard to raise them to a fair price later because a 'fee anchor' has now been set down in their mind. So, start them out right in the first place.

Myth 10: Last year's fee is a good guide for this year's fee.

Reality: Things are almost always different; the client just is not aware of the differences.

Why? That's easy – because you do not tell them.

Myth 11: Paying your invoice is as high a priority for your client as getting paid is for you.

Reality: Some clients don't pay simply because they have not been asked to.

And, since most accountants do not charge interest on overdue accounts, it costs clients nothing to delay settlement. Set the right expectations with your clients from day one.

Myth 12: If you charge lower prices than the competition, you will get more clients *and* they will pay their invoices.

Reality: Clients do not know what their accountant's competitors charge, nor do they care.

In fact, most accountants also do not know what their competitors charge.

To the extent that you are able, maybe over a period of 12 months, find out about four of your worthy competitors their:

- Highest owner charge out rate
- Lowest owner charge out rate
- Standard charge out rate for £25,000 employee
- Standard charge out rate for bookkeeping or accounts preparation
- Standard charge out rate for accounts staff
- Realisation percent (or write-down).

Myth 13: The client's gratitude for the good job you did endures after you finish the job.

Reality: Clients quickly forget what their accountant did for them.

Roger Dawson in the Secrets of Power Negotiating states, "The value of a service rendered declines rapidly once the service is completed."

That's why you should send your invoices as soon as possible after a service is complete.

Myth 14: Further, clients appreciate it when you delay sending them their invoices.

Reality: Clients want to know how much they owe even if they can't pay right now.

You should invoice promptly because WIP depreciates.

Myth 15: Slow payment is the price of keeping clients.

Reality: Clients will respect you if you make them pay. They will not if you don't.

Myth 16: Asking clients to pay is unprofessional.

Reality: Not asking clients to pay is unprofessional.

Clients will appreciate you more as a business adviser if you run your practice in a business-like professional manner. Invoicing promptly and holding clients accountable to your payment terms sends the right message about your firm as business advisers.

Would you use a family doctor who was obese or out of shape?

Myth 17: If you do ask clients to pay, they will take their business elsewhere.

Reality: If they are not paying, they are not a client.

Myth 18: The client sitting in your office right now is the last client you will ever get.

Therefore: (a) you better not make the client angry by asking for a fee in advance payment; (b) you better take whatever the client is willing to pay you because something is better than nothing.

Reality: The world is full of clients. The Rule of SW3: "Some will. Some won't. So what?" Walk-away power. You should always retain walk away power.

Myth 19: The amount recorded on your time management system indicates the fair price.

Reality: Any relationship between the amount of work-in-progress (WIP) and the true value of the job may be only coincidental.

The amount on your time management system only indicates what you invested in an engagement at your standard charge rate. It has little or nothing to do with the value of the work.

Myth 20: When you or your team make a mistake, you should write off the time involved.

Reality: Mistakes are part of life and part of business.

If you or your team never made mistakes your charge out rates would be much higher. The fact that you make mistakes is reflected in your charge out rate; likewise for your employees. Their salary and charge out rates reflect their levels of experience and performance.

If someone makes a mistake, the time is still chargeable. They should note in the time report that a mistake was made, but charge it anyway. Elsewhere in the engagement, they (or someone else) might be super-efficient and finish in less time than you thought. You may be able to charge for all your costs. If not, the write-down reflects how well you managed your costs.

Myth 21: What you do cannot be very valuable, because it is easy for you.

Reality: The things that come easy to accountants are impossible for the clients.

Do any of these myths sound familiar?

These myths cost accountants thousands of pounds every day. And they are shooting themselves in the foot.

These myths are not imposed by law or ethics, only by attitudes. (There's that word *attitude* again) These myths subconsciously remain in the background of most accountants' thinking and the forefront of their habits. Thus, they remain in place until accountants consciously change them.

I do not know whether these myths were ever true, but they are not true today. How many of these do *you* unconsciously accept?

Module 3
Top line management

Five factors that affect your prices

Only five things affect the amount you can charge for your services:

1. Demand for what you do

2. How easily someone can replace you

3. Your ability – or efficiency

4. Return on investment of resources – or effectiveness

Effectiveness is 'doing the right things right'. An individual's resource is his or her time. A firm's resource is employee and owner time. Owners improve their ROI with better time management, delegation, supervision of team members, and better client selection and client management.

5. The fifth factor…

The willingness to demand it. Have the courage to demand what you are worth.

The key is top line management

1. Enhancing revenue instead of reducing costs

2. Not compromising on prices

How to make 'balanced' changes

You can increase *effective* charge out rates by maintaining the same realisation and increasing your average standard charge out rate or by maintaining the same standard charge out rates and increasing realisation. Often, the best way to produce a desired increase in effective charge out rates with the least change in operations is to make balanced changes in *each* of the two factors.

Current realisation less than 85%

If your current realisation is less than 85%, I would agree that an increase in charge out rates may not be appropiate, provided you target an immediate increase in realisation of at least 5%.

Current realisation above 85%

If your current realisation is at or above 85%, your entire increase in effective charge out rates should be from higher charge out rates. Let your realisation remain where it is or even drift down a little to the low 80s. My empirical observation is that the highest effective charge out rates seem to be achieved with higher standard charge out rates and realisation in the low 80s.

If you do it the right way, you can normally increase charge out rates 10 to 15% for employees and 10 to 20% for some owners without clients even noticing the change.

Module 4
Setting prices

There are different ways for accountants to price their services:

- Cost-plus pricing
- Fixed pricing
- Results pricing
- Value pricing
- Combinations of the above

Variations of *cost-plus* pricing are the most common in the profession. The accounting firm starts with their direct labour costs, adds an overhead factor and a profit factor, and assigns standard charge out rates to each person in the firm based on their hourly pay. Owner rates are set subjectively somewhat higher than the rates of the most experienced employees. The most junior owners typically have rates about 30 percent higher than the typical manager. The average owner charge out rate is three to four times that of a recent graduate with less than one year of experience.

Fixed-price agreements are contracts to provide specific services to clients for a fixed price, regardless of the accountant's cost to perform them. These are often used for pricing bundles of related services such as bookkeeping, financial statements, and tax returns for a single client

Results pricing is the practice of agreeing with the client *in advance* to charge based on the results you obtain, regardless of your costs incurred. Commissions and contingent prices are examples of results pricing. You might consider *results pricing* if you help a client sell their business or save the client a large amount of tax, e.g. secure a favourable result at a VAT tribunal or save IHT or other taxes.

In *value pricing,* the price may not be set until after the engagement is finished in order to evaluate the accountant's contribution and invoice accordingly. Most accountants have done this – at least when evaluating their contribution *downward* – for many years.

Key point: To clients every bill is viewed as a value bill. Clients always adopt a so-called 'value pricing' approach. Unless they feel they received value from you greater than the price, they will be unhappy with your invoice.

Cost-driven prices versus value-driven prices

Most accountants determine prices by multiplying the time spent by staff at charge out rate for each person or for that type of service. We refer to these types of prices as *cost driven* because the amount of cost incurred performing an engagement directly affects the amount invoiced to the client.

Other accountants base their prices on the value of the results obtained rather than on the costs involved to perform the service.

Example: If the result is disappointing, the accountant will take a write-down or sometimes no fee at all, regardless of the amount of time invested in the engagement. If the results are very good, the accountant will invoice the client more than standard rates.

We call these prices *value driven*, and they are common in other professions such as estate agency, investment management and health care. The accounting profession has some cost-driven prices and some value-driven prices, with a predominance of cost-driven prices.

Example: An accountant's price to prepare a routine financial statement is based principally on the time involved. But the price to represent a client in a dispute with tax authorities could be based on the amount of taxes saved.

The overwhelming majority of accounting practices record all time charges to clients as work-in-progress (WIP) at an amount based on standard charge out rates for each person.

When engagements are completed and invoiced, any difference between the standard revenue amount and the final amount invoiced is recognised as a write-down or write-up.

Pricing and risk

Cost-plus pricing transfers risk to the client. This cuts both ways. Although accountants prefer to have clients take the risk of the job going over budget or unforeseen engagement problems (which is what cost-plus pricing does), clients prefer the accountants to take the risk. After all, accountants are the professionals and they should know what they are doing.

Profit comes from risk. No risk, no reward.

When you transfer risk to your clients, they will seek to limit your reward. That's only fair. If you adopt value pricing, you assume more risk, but you expect greater rewards. That's fair, too.

Just as cost-plus pricing transfers risk to the client, fixed-price agreements and, to various degrees, other value-driven pricing transfers risk to the accountant. In return for assuming the risk, the accountant charges a risk premium to the client by pricing at above standard charge rates. The client gains a ceiling on price.

Aligning the accountant's interests with those of the client

Key point: Cost-plus pricing creates an inevitable conflict of interest with clients.

By making hours important, you encourage the client to focus on hours instead of results. And since you may well charge a standard charge out rate several times higher than your client makes per hour, you force them to focus on your hours.

Setting prices

If your clients focus on hours, they constantly try to figure whether they can afford you and ignore the value you provide. The multidimensional value you create is turned, like gold into lead, into a one-dimensional, commoditised, easily compared price.

- Cost-plus pricing focuses on efforts, not results.
- Cost-plus pricing doesn't reward creativity and innovation; it rewards inexperience and inefficiency, even incompetence.
- Cost-plus pricing has its advantages. It's easy to explain to clients. It's easy to administer. It's easy to defend. And it is a great retail cost-accounting tool.
- Cost-plus pricing encourages people to work harder, not smarter, by reducing incentives to creatively increase productivity. It penalises investments in technology. Some accounting firms hesitated to invest in software systems to facilitate the production of tax returns and financial statements. Was this partly because they were concerned their fees would decline because of the decrease in chargeable hours? Cost-plus pricing encourages the accumulation of hours while budgeting seeks to define hours that are perceived as acceptable or even desirable. Cost-plus pricing can also discourage delegation.

Whenever you use cost-plus pricing, you will have write-downs.

How to set prices

To set the right prices, you have to know your cost to service each client and your cost to provide each type of service. There is a limit on how long you can provide a service that costs you more than clients are willing to pay.

Key point: Use your time recording system as a retail cost accounting system.

Your time recording system may or possibly should provide:

- Productivity information by person, including chargeable hours, total hours, and comparison to target on a weekly or monthly basis
- Realisation information by person, including the net effective charge out rate attained after allocating write-downs to personnel who worked on the engagement, net revenue produced, and comparison to target monthly
- Proper allocation of time charges to clients
- Proper allocation of write-downs to clients
- Daily time reporting
- Automatic input verification of client numbers, charge codes, and employee numbers
- Grouping related clients and treating them as one client for analysis purposes
- Printing a list of clients and related cost and fee information sorted by fees (ascending or descending), realisation (ascending and descending), and absolute size of write-downs (ascending and descending)
- Exporting appropriate files to your spreadsheet program.

Some accountants may look at the above criteria and think they will need to invest in new time management software. Actually, your current time recording system may provide most of these features. It might provide all, but you need to study the operating manual.

Chargeable time or billable time?

Chargeable time is time spent that is identifiable with serving a particular client, regardless of whether or not the client is ultimately invoiced for all of the time. Chargeable time measures the standard cost of serving each client.

Since accounting firms record their time at standard charge out rates which include a standard profit, some accountants, and especially less-experienced employees, are confused about the distinction between *chargeable* time and *billable* time based on whether they intend to send an invoice for the service.

This confusion causes some professionals to think that, if they are not going to invoice the client for the charges, they should not record the time.

This is a major cause of lack of profitability, because failing to record all chargeable time or other cost distorts the cost records for that client. The next time you have to set a price or make a budget, you don't know how much it cost to do the job last year, and your pricing decisions are less accurate.

Charging time to a client is not the same as *invoicing* a client. These are two different management decisions:

- First, what does it cost to perform this service for the client?
- Next, how should I price this service?

Occasionally you may perform a service and choose not to invoice the client for whatever reason. Nevertheless, the time spent performing that service is a *cost of serving that client* which you should know in order to make better decisions.

Some accountants routinely reduce or increase their time before invoicing. These accountants often decide as they record their time how much they will invoice for the work.

If they don't intend to invoice the client for the work, they will not charge the time to work in progress (WIP). For example, if they intend not to invoice the client for looking up an item in the file, copying it, and sending the client the copy, they record the time in a non chargeable category (or do not record it at all). On another project, they might work ten hours at £150 per hour but intend to give the client a discount. So, they only record eight hours. Again, *this is a major cause of lack of profitability* because these accountants lose track of the true cost of serving such clients.

On the other hand, if they spend 15 minutes looking up some research they had previously done in three hours for another client, they may record three 'billable' hours for 15 minutes work, thus using the time recording system to record the price that they intend to invoice. But this distorts the cost and profitability of serving that client.

Non chargeable time is time worked that is not chargeable to a client. This includes training, recruiting, professional meetings, practice development, administration, and firm meetings, no matter whether the time is spent during regular business hours or not. It also includes community activities, holidays, and authorised leaves of absence during business hours.

Key point: The criterion for whether time is chargeable is: If I did not have this client, would I have spent this time doing something else? If the answer is *yes*, the time is chargeable.

There is another danger in making pricing decisions at the time you record your time: Your employees will follow your example. They will usurp *your* pricing decisions by deciding whether or not to record time spent serving clients. If you don't know the time was spent, you never get the chance to make the pricing decision. Again, *this is a major cause of lack of profitability!*

Key point: The single most important type of information you, as a manager, need is, *"How much does it cost me to serve each and every client?"*

When to use value pricing

Value pricing means pricing your services based on their value to your client, rather than on your cost to provide them. You can and should price many engagements based on value to the client rather than time spent.

I recommend value pricing when the primary *value-driver* of the engagement is *knowledge, skill* or *experience*, rather than the routine application of time and technology to routine problems. Most tax, planning, and consulting services should be priced on value rather than your time cost.

The value gap

Key point: Often, clients *do not know* what your services are worth.

Key point: Often, accountants also do not know what their services are worth.

Key point: The *Value Gap* is the amount which clients are willing to pay in excess of the amount which the accountant has the courage to charge.

Most clients are willing to pay a fair price. Clients periodically need to be reassured that the firm's pricing policy is fair – maybe not the cheapest – but fair.

Determining value to the client

Once you know or can estimate your cost to complete an engagement, you should determine the value of that service to the client.

Remember these three key points:

1. All value is subjective; the client's assignment of value will probably be very different from your valuation.

2. The buyer of a service always values it higher than the seller.

3. You, as a seller, will value the service lower than the seller.

If the client's valuation is higher than yours, he or she will not tell you because their role as an economic consumer is to buy things at the least cost.

Key point: Determine the client's assessment of the value of the service before you discuss price.

Key point: Prices should be based on perceived value to the client, assuming the value is higher than the accountant's cost to provide the service.

The buyer's perception of value is the first thing you need to determine on all non-routine services. Accountants are usually remiss in not obtaining some agreement with the client on the value of the project and the nature of that value. You just charge ahead without even discussing the value. (Remember Commandmyth number one?)

We recommend asking a selection of the following questions to establish value for the client.

- What will be different about your company (or your situation) at the conclusion of this project?
- What would happen if you did nothing?
- What if this project failed (or have these attempts failed in the past)?
- What will you be able to do that you can't do now?
- What will be the effect on revenue (profits, market share, personnel, and so forth)?
- What will be the three greatest impacts of this project's success? (people love to think in threes!)
- What will this mean to you personally?
- What peripheral and secondary value do you see from this project?
- What will you be proudest of at the conclusion of this project?

From these and similar discussions you can obtain an understanding of the client's perception of value.

Key point: To get the client's commitment to a fair price you must agree on three things:

Objectives for the project: What are the business, financial, and personal outcomes the client expects? Be as specific as possible.

Metrics: How will the client know if those objectives are achieved?

Value: The client's statement of how he or she and their business and/or family will be better off with those objectives being met.

Factors affecting your value

Besides objective elements, such as time at standard charge out rates and other direct chargeable expenses, you should consider subjective factors that warrant a price either higher or lower than standard.

For routine work, you can start with time charges at standard to determine the amount to invoice. After all, standard time charges reflect your costs in the engagement (plus a normal profit), and you have to recover your costs. The real criterion is the value to clients. Too often, accountants recognise this value only negatively by invoicing at less than standard charge out rates. In other words, they will take write-downs but not write ups. Subjective factors affecting pricing include:

- *Special capabilities, skill, and professional expertise of the persons doing the work.* A person's standard charge out rate for a service may not reflect their special expertise in a specific industry. Even though a manager's regular rate for consulting is, say £150, if he or she has special experience in the client's industry, that would make him or her more valuable or efficient, you can justify a higher rate than standard.

- *Degree of risk and responsibility assumed.* Special services, such as the purchase or sale of a business and certain types of tax, business consulting, and specialist services merit higher prices. Likewise, if you face special risks (such as the possibility of not getting paid if a startup company fails), you can charge a risk premium. If you supervise a multidisciplinary team, or otherwise carry greater than normal responsibility, you should charge more. The intended use of the accountant's report, and the possibility of liability also may indicate the risk and responsibility of the services rendered.

- *Seasonal factors.* Using dual charge out rates has some of the effect of seasonal pricing, since a great deal of the work on preparation of tax returns is performed in the last two months before the filing deadline. Firms are going to have to evaluate how the tax staff will be utilised from 1 December to 31 March. Should work in this period be charged at an 'off-season discount', thus charge out rates are discounted from 6 April to 30 November and increased from 1 December to 5 April. Or, should tax staff be hired only for eight months? Or should tax staff be retrained?

- *Value of services to the client.* Logically, prices should directly relate to the value of the service performed for the client. And that value should also reflect the degree of risk involved, and the nature of the services. Often, standard time charges for a service do not correspond to the value of the service to the client. The most obvious situations include negotiating a higher sales price or a lower purchase price for a client, savings in taxes, increases in profitability, strategic planning, obtaining financing, as well as occasions when you help a client increase their top line. A complicated tax settlement may depend on the accountant's thorough knowledge and judicious reasoning with HMRC to gain a substantial saving for the client. Remember that it is knowledge that creates the 'value' in the value of the services, not time.

Key point: The amounts involved, *i.e.* the size of the transaction, also indicate the value

- *The results obtained.* Results are important in contingent prices or results pricing. Contingent prices are not necessarily allowed in all engagements or by all professional bodies. But even in regular engagements, you may subjectively consider the results you achieved for the client.
- *Priority and importance of the work to the client.* If the client asks to 'jump the queue' and have you reschedule appointments or delay work for other clients to make room for their project, the price should reflect these special arrangements.
- *Loss of access to other markets.* If you have a client who doesn't want you working with their competitor, or if you agree a contingent price with a client that depends on increases in the client's profits, you might be precluded from working with that client's competitors or from performing assurance type services. If so, you should charge a premium price because you are foregoing other opportunities.
- *Lack of ability to pay.* If it makes sense to make allowances for widows and charities (and it does makes sense to most of you), then it is also fair to make judicious upward adjustments if the client's financial condition warrants.
- *Special efforts required.* If you worked all weekend on an otherwise routine engagement because the client had an emergency, you should charge extra. Such extra charges are normal in business. Customers pay a premium for convenience and overtime for faster service.
- *Difficulty of the engagement.* If you had to move heaven and earth to accomplish the engagement, you deserve a bonus. Also, consider the time limits imposed by the client or the circumstances.
- *Length of time you have been involved with the client.* A client whom you have served for many years would deserve more consideration than a one-shot client who came to you for one high-value consulting service but who remained the regular client of another firm. On the other hand, working for a client with whom you have 'earned your spurs' means you are much more effective because of your long familiarity with the client's affairs, and you can create value more easily than with a newer client. That is why long-standing clients will accept a higher price than new ones because the old clients know you will do an excellent job.
- *Acceptability of the price (both to you and the client).* It makes no economic sense for you to charge a client £3,000 for an engagement that saved him or her only £2,000; it likewise makes little sense for you to invoice a client £5,000 for an engagement that saved him or her £100,000.
- Certain types of engagements usually deserve pricing above standard: tax investigations, financial planning, investment advice, tax planning strategies, engagements that increase the client's profits, and negotiating the purchase or sale of a business.
- These engagements may have characteristics such as the following:

1. Often, the client can measure the benefit, such as reduction in a proposed tax liability, purchase or sale price for a business, profitability increase, etc. Usually, the client does not have the necessary skill to do the work himself or herself

2. The client may have the skill but not the time. They may have no one else in the company to fill in. If you represent a £200,000-a-year executive and free up his or her time to pursue other pressing interests, that certainly deserves more than £200 an hour!

3. The engagement is non-routine, requiring high-level technical skill, business acumen, or mature judgement

4. Client's sensitivity about the project

5. Rules of thumb followed by others in similar circumstances

6. The amount of money involved is relatively large.

Key point: Clients accept value pricing better than most accountants do, *if* – and *only* if – you discuss the price with them *before* you perform the service.

When to use results pricing

Other professions such as brokerage, investment management, real estate conveyance, and personal injury cases base prices on results, usually defined as a percentage of the amounts involved.

Results pricing is the practice of agreeing with the client *in advance* to charge based on the results you obtain, regardless of your costs incurred. Commissions and contingent prices are examples of results pricing.

Results pricing is not a gratuity you add on for extra special service. That is value pricing.

It is not invoicing a £1,656 engagement for £1,750. That is normal invoicing practice.

Results pricing is not 'getting lucky' by being able to charge extra after an engagement is completed. You thought the research would take £1,500 of time and you found the answer in one hour. That is value pricing.

It *may be* 'standard prices plus a bonus' if the bonus is based on results.

Example: You can price business accounting/invoice paying services based on the number of transactions, *i.e.*, invoices you process. Or you could price this service on the amount of money involved, *i.e.*, £volume of deposits made or cheques prepared. Or both. Both bases reflect the value involved, yet neither necessarily reflects the time required.

You must position yourself for a results-based invoice by discussing the situation with the client *in advance*. Explain why it is worth what it is worth. Explain how you will contribute value to the client. And discuss the basis for your price. Explain that you bring unique skills that the client may not be able to get any other way.

Key point: You cannot control the client's perception of your value *retroactively*. You must do it at the outset.

Use results pricing when the results are objectively measurable and the value to the client has little or nothing to do with the amount of time you require to do the job.

When to use fixed-price agreements

Fixed-price agreements transfer risk from the client to the accountant. In return for assuming the risk, you can charge a risk premium to the client by pricing at more than your standard rates. Many clients, given a choice, prefer to pay a little more in return for having a ceiling on their price.

1. Start with your estimated time at standard charge out rates

2. Then add at least a 20-percent contingency because you are too optimistic when you budget

3. Next, add the risk premium you earn by taking the risk off the client's shoulders

4. Finally, add any premium you want from bundling your services into packages.

Fixed-price agreements communicate confidence. An upfront quote projects confidence, experience, and competence on your part. It also contains the seeds of disaster, if you are not careful.

How long could a restaurateur remain in business if he or she said, "I will feed you for £250 a month?" How long would it take before customers began to come in every day, and then every meal? Soon they would begin to order lobster and expensive wine.

Yet accountants do the same thing. They quote a client a monthly retainer or fixed price for an engagement and do not specify what the engagement includes and – more importantly – does *not* include. Then they get sucked in to doing more and more work each month.

We will discuss this phenomenon later.

To avoid this disaster, the fixed-price agreement must specifically cover what you will do and then state that any additional work will be the subject of another agreement or a *variation order*.

Example: Builders always charge for extras. Often they require a signed variation order.

We should learn from the example of builders. Accountants might also include 'specifications and plans' in their agreements.

Example: I once had a client whose audit grew over the years to over 200 hours. I never missed budget by more than 2 percent, because I attached an appendix to the engagement letter specifying all the work their personnel would do and its due dates. And each week I met with the client to review progress and make adjustments to both the budget and the price as the work progressed.

When I discuss reducing write-downs in a later module, I will cover the subject of planning conferences with both the client and your engagement team.

If the builder's customer wants an extra, the builder has leverage because they have already started the job and are familiar with it. The cost for the customer to switch builders would be prohibitive at this stage. If you have property clients, you probably know that some builders even lowball a bid and count on the variation orders to provide all the profit in their job.

How to raise prices

Suppose, after this studying *Defining Edge* Practice Management Strategies, you decide your prices are too low. (Note that although this programme uses the term *raise prices*, when you discuss prices with clients, you never *raise prices*, you always *adjust prices*.)

Q: So, how do you raise them?

A: You raise prices by raising prices.

Example: You charged Tina Taxpayer £565 last year, and you think she should pay £650 this year. Just do the work, and invoice her £650. That's only about a 15 percent increase. Most people have no problem with increases of less than 10 to 15 percent.

Example: You charged Jeremy Client £465 last year, but, after looking back at the value of what you did, you think you should have charged £700. If Jeremy's past record holds, this year will be even more complicated, perhaps to a fair price of £800 or more.

After Jeremy brings in his information this year – but before you start work on it – you say, "Jeremy, I went back and looked at what we charged you last year and I realise that we should have charged you £700 for the work we did. Also, we have made some adjustments to our prices since last year. This year, it looks like the price for your return will be about £800, assuming it is no more complicated than last year. If it is more complicated, the price may be higher. Because this is significantly higher than we have charged you in the past, I wanted you to know about this price adjustment."

If Jeremy has a problem with a £750 or £800 price, it is better for you to find out before doing the work. This gives him the opportunity to take his business elsewhere, and gives you the opportunity to stop working for less than you are worth.

4th session

Module 5
Discussing prices with clients

Many accountants somehow have the idea that it is unprofessional to discuss prices with clients. Perhaps they think it gives clients the wrong impression that the accountant is primarily concerned with money. Yet no one wants to buy something with no idea of the price.

When you go into a store, who brings up the subject of price? The store. They do it by attaching price tags to everything. When you go to a garage, who first mentions the price? The petrol station. They post their prices on signs and on the pumps. These are the signs that have told us all just how much fuel has increased in recent years. When you are interested in buying a building, who starts the price negotiation? The seller does, by listing an asking price.

Key point: If goods and services are being sold, the seller has the responsibility to mention the price first.

Even if the price will be subject to negotiation – such as property or used cars – the seller opens the negotiation with an asking price.

For people whose very language of business is money, accountants demonstrate an amazing reluctance to discuss prices.

Key point: Many clients are embarrassed to mention price because they believe it will make them appear unsophisticated. They are relieved when you bring up the subject.

If the accountant is also too embarrassed to discuss prices, a disaster could be waiting for both accountant and client. As mentioned earlier…

Key point: Clients accept value pricing better than most accountants do – *if* – and *only* if – you discuss the price with them *before* you perform the service.

Whether you discuss prices or not, the client has some price in mind. It's hard enough to meet a client's expectation if you know them; it's impossible if you don't even know what price range they are considering. Therefore, it's just good business to discuss price with clients before committing any firm resources to the project.

Key point: Avoid the word *fee* when speaking to clients, prospects, and referral sources. Instead, say *price*. People sometimes perceive *fees* to be more negotiable than *prices*.

This section covers how to get off on the right foot with a new client, the client's point of view when discussing price, guidelines on how to communicate price, and how to handle specific problems, such as objections and complaints.

Train your clients to pay you well and promptly

What "How much is this going to cost?" really means

When clients enquire regarding the cost of the service they are most likely seeking to establish what they should budget, or if this is a service they can afford. It is easy to hear a subliminal message that this is, perhaps, a service they cannot afford or that you are too expensive. For some it takes courage to ask a professional what it will cost, but given that, mostly accountancy services can't be compared, we should answer the question by giving the client an estimate range and indicate the proviso(s) with regard to the lower end estimate. Your pricing communicates your value.

If you price your services at the low end of the market, clients won't take you seriously. If you are expensive, not only will they respect you, they are more likely to implement your recommendations because they paid so much for them.

Example: When I first went into practice, Bob Bennett, a very successful managing partner in Bristol, taught me to answer the question, "How much do you charge?" by saying "We are as expensive as anyone, and our clients think we are worth it".

Key point: The more people pay for something, the more valuable it is.

Naturally, you should always discuss price before you perform a service. This is not only common courtesy; it is also good business. You have greater leverage with a client before you perform a service because the client wants something from you (a solution to a problem). After you perform the service, the client has greater leverage because you want something from the client (money).

One important factor affecting the client's perception of your value is your own attitude toward your prices. Just as some animals can 'smell fear', clients can often sense if you are uncomfortable with your own prices. They observe – often unconsciously – your tone of voice, the words you choose, the loudness of your voice, your body language, even your breathing. If you are ambivalent or wishy-washy, a good negotiator will sense that and press the advantage to lower your prices.

On the other hand, if you are comfortable with your value and your prices, clients will also sense that and they, too, will feel confidence in your value. I learned this simple truth from one of my own clients.

Key point: What you say with confidence, they will believe!

Most clients will pay a fair price. They are chiefly concerned that other clients pay comparable prices. Clients periodically need reassurance that the firm charges all its clients fairly – maybe not cheaply, but fairly.

How to use Lloydbottom's law and Lloydbottom's corollary

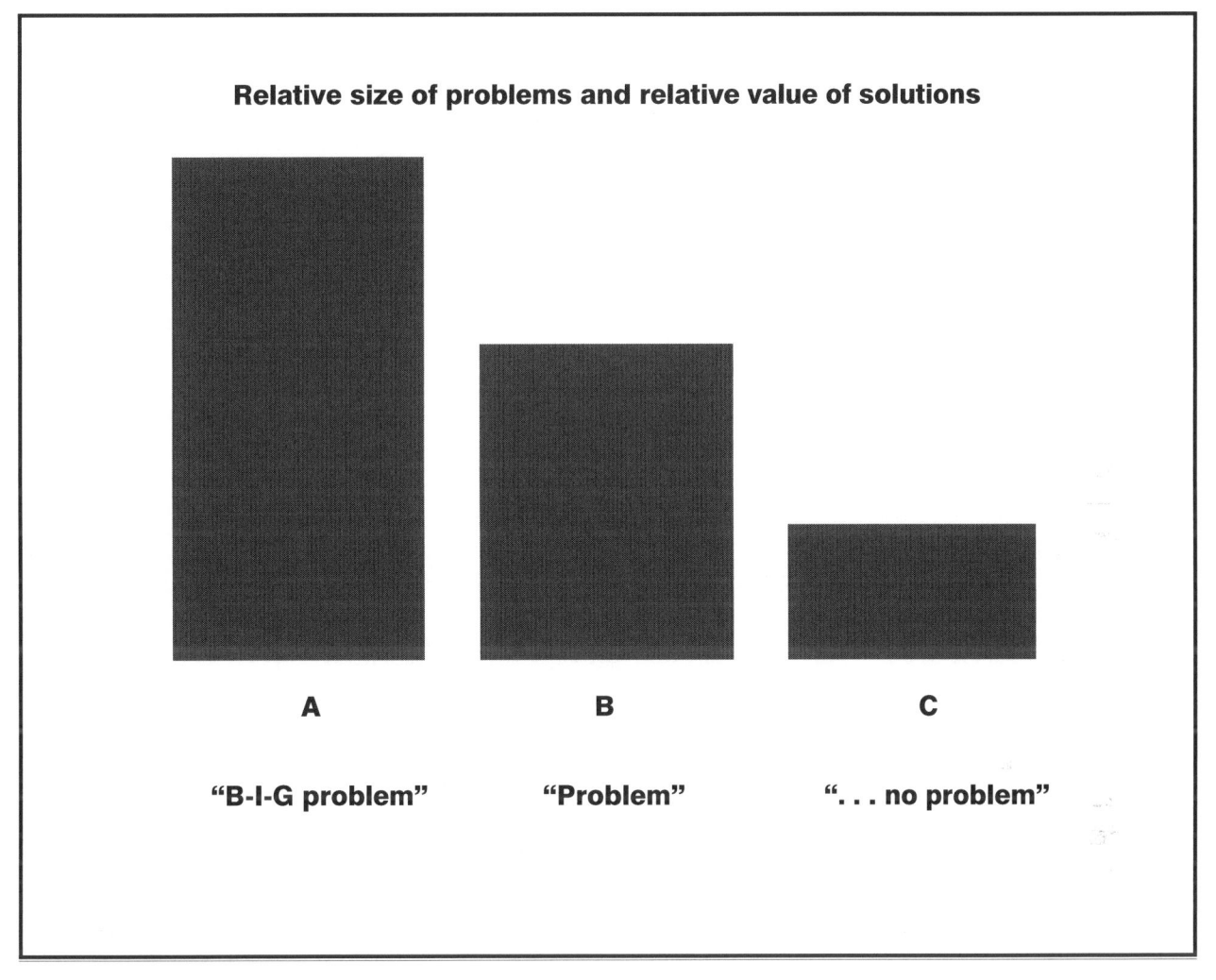

Relative size of problems and relative value of solutions

A	B	C
"B-I-G problem"	"Problem"	"... no problem"

Key point: A client's problem is always bigger to the client than it is to you.

Key point: Lloydbottom's law: The value of the solution varies with the size of problem.

Key point: Lloydbottom's corollary: The bigger the problem, the more valuable the solution.

Key point: If you minimise the size of the problem, you minimise the value of your solution.

The problem with price estimates

Price estimates are just that, but accountants often fail to communicate that to clients. Clients are given the impression that an estimate is a fixed price even though that was not what was intended. Even a regular client, who understands that your quote is only an estimate, will eventually lose confidence if the final prices consistently exceeds the estimates.

Accountants are usually better off estimating a project on the high side and then giving the client a pleasant surprise. Then they will learn that the estimate is usually a worst case.

The danger, especially with new clients, is that a high estimate will, in fact, prompt them to look elsewhere. So, they never become regular clients.

To prevent this, accountants should give the estimate as a range, carefully explain all the variables, and explain to the client what he or she can do to help keep the price low.

How to avoid professional panic

Some accountants get panicked by what is going on in the lowest 10 percent of the market.

Key point: Focus on the 90-plus percent of your clients who are very happy with your prices and your service. You never hear from them about how reasonable they think your prices are, so you often forget they are there.

Ask for an advance payment – a deposit

Always ask for a payment in advance from a new client as an evidence of his or her commitment to the relationship. If clients are unwilling to pay a portion of your price before the service, he or she may be unwilling to pay after the service. An up front payment requirement also serves as part of the screening process for new clients.

Be flexible

Be flexible in your terms and make it easy to buy. For instance, it's okay to take credit cards. Most clients who engage you don't have cash-flow problems, but occasionally one will have a problem with a request for a deposit to confirm your engagement. If your conflict of interest checks and due diligence disclose no other problems with the client, you may accommodate him or her. As long as your clients pay the agreed price for your yearly services over the year you deliver them, I don't see a problem. For instance, if you are negotiating with a retailer who is cash-strapped in a particular season, they may prefer to match their payments to their cash flow. Some people prefer to pay monthly or quarterly, depending on when their customers pay them.

Important tools in negotiating prices...

Who initiated the need? If the client called you, you can charge more.

1. The eyebrow test

2. The anchoring effect

3. Ask "How much have you budgeted to solve this problem?" Ask the client what the price should be, or how much it is worth. Value is in the eyes of the client. If he or

she sees £1,000 of value for a job that will cost £15,000 to do, better find out before you do the job.

4. If I can save you £5,000, how much of the savings/extra money/etc. are you willing to share with me?"

How to handle price objections

Never sell on price or cut your fee. Once you do that, they will never be good clients.

Instead, just ask:

"Do you know what it will cost you if you don't do it?"

For estate planning, you may joke that it won't cost them anything; it will cost their kids.

If the client continues to object, say this:

"Our fee is a minor investment compared to what you can save (or make or gain)."

This again places their attention on results instead of the cost.

Then, go into what they will gain, depending on the nature of the engagement. Whether the service will be succession planning, retirement planning, a new accounting system, or whatever, you should paint a vivid picture for the client of how rosy the future can be if they solve this problem.

Alternatively, you might also paint a picture of how bad it could be if they do not solve the problem.

Keep them thinking about what they will gain or save, not about your price.

"If you neglect tax planning, it's like saying you would rather HMRC get your money than yourself or your own children and grandchildren."

How to handle procrastinators

Some clients don't like to make decisions. They will say "I have to study the issue and sleep on it before I make a decision," or "I'm going on holidays. I'll do it later," or "I am very busy for the next eight weeks. Let's talk about it when I'm freed up."

Here is a selection of concerns you could express:

"If anything happens to you between now and then, I would hate myself for letting you delay. Changes in your circumstances could foreclose some options you now have; they would no longer be available. The longer you wait, the more risk you take that you will be left with fewer choices. You may lose a key employee, your building could catch fire, you could become uninsurable, you might get disabled. Who knows what the future holds? You will sleep better at night once you handle this. Do it now."

How to handle price complaints

How many of your clients are *really* complaining?

- Make sure it is a complaint and not a comment.
- "Who knows? Maybe he will lower the price. It cannot hurt to ask."

For *real* complaints, ask

- "Why do you think it is too high?"

Nine out of ten times, when a client does complain about a price, the price is not the real problem, say

- "Evaluate us over one to two years."
- "We are worth three times what we cost."

Allow for value pricing in your engagement letters

You can and should invoice many routine engagements based on value to the client rather than time charges. Even in routine engagements, allow for value pricing in the engagement letter terms.

Unfortunately many firms' standard engagement letter terms do not allow for invoicing above standard charge out rates, even where justified. Instead they will include a price provision such as: "Our prices are based on the time we devote to an engagement."

Here is appropriate illustrative language:

Example: We generally base our prices on the time required at our regular charge out rates for the services and personnel assigned plus out-of-pocket costs [Note the use of the word *generally* which allows for exceptions.]

Example: However, our charges also might include other appropriate factors, including the difficulty of the assignment, how much risk and responsibility the work entails, time limitations imposed on us by others, the experience and professional expertise of the personnel assigned, and the priority and importance of the work to the client.

Example: Assuming adequate records, internal controls, and assistance of your personnel, we estimate that our price for the [services] will range between £_____ and £_____. We will attempt to minimise our charges without sacrificing the quality of our work. The extent to which this can be done will depend on the availability of your personnel to offer us clerical and other assistance in preparing schedules, performing analyses, and providing source documents. If we encounter any significant unusual circumstances not contemplated in preparing the estimate, we will discuss it with you and arrive at a new price estimate before we incur additional costs. [Accountants often omit these contingencies from engagement letters, making it easy for the client's personnel to avoid helping the accountant.]

Example: These estimated prices are based on the assumption that you will continue to employ competent, experienced bookkeeping personnel. If a change in your personnel requires us to spend extra time to train your people or otherwise perform our services, we will invoice you for such extra time. [You might use this language for a client who has had high staff turnover in the accounting department.]

When value pricing opportunities arise, discuss the price with the client *before* you begin work and obtain his or her agreement about how you will invoice the engagement. One of our clients obtained a £10,000 write up on one engagement by following this recommendation.

Delivering results – getting paid what you're worth – 5th session

Module 1
21 ways to improve your billing

The typical accounting firm invoicing procedures includes some or many of these characteristics:

- Owners do the invoicing, or at least approve all invoices before clients see them.
- They invoice based on standard time charges plus some out-of-pocket expenses.
- They send invoices after the engagement is finished – sometimes long after.
- Even progress invoices are sent only after the engagement is well begun and much of the cost is incurred.
- Often, the entire invoice is sent only after the engagement is complete.
- Clients don't know the price of the engagement in advance. But, they will nevertheless have a definite idea of what the price should be.
- Even though the firm completes an engagement in the early part of the month, the invoice goes out after the first of the following month – again, sometimes long after.
- Time records are supposed to be updated daily, but they are frequently late, especially from the owners.
- WIP runs are delayed for several days after the end of the accounting period, often because of missing time or expense reports from owners.
- Some owners don't invoice on the first day the WIP is available.

Do any of these characteristics look familiar?

Key point: The more of these characteristics you have in your firm, the more trouble you will have making money.

1. Use the 50-minute hour

Key point: My personal interviews and reviews of firm owners' time sheets show that some people charge at least one hour or more a day to various non chargeable activities, *even when fully occupied all day long on chargeable work*!

Most firms set their charge out rates on the (unstated) assumption that the seven and a half hour day generates seven and a half hour chargeable hours. They just do not explain that to the employees and all the owners.

The following nine points cover 21 opportunities/reasons to improve your billing.

2. Round up, not down

Key point: Round up all invoices over £1,000 to the next £100. Round up all invoices between £500 and £949 to the next £50. Round up invoices less than £474 to the next £25

What would be the effect if each of those were rounded up instead of down? The answer may be as many as 400 invoices a year times £50, or £20,000 a year for each owner!

3. Use the underachievers list

One of my clients developed a list of what they called 'underachievers' – specific clients who yielded less than a certain percentage of realisation. The list was circulated to all owners each month and owners began to take a great deal of pride in getting clients for whom they were responsible off the list.

Do you compile a list of clients in descending order of profitability?

If not, could you?

What reports on client profitability and profitability by firm owner do you monitor/manage?

To whom do you distribute those reports?

What action is taken?

4. Use peer pressure

You can increase realisation by getting firm owners to invoice more. It sounds simple, and it is. But simple does not always mean easy.

One of my clients increased realisation seven percent in just four months by the simple expedient of passing out each owner's billings each month. Peer pressure did the rest.

What forms of peer pressure could you use in your firm?

5. Require second owner approval on sub-standard invoices

We showed one client how to get their partners to invoice more. With no increase in new business, no change in costs, no improvement in efficiency, using this simple procedure, they began charging more for the same work and increased their realisation from 87% to 95% in less than a year. **The average owner's income increased by 15 percent.** Here is how they did it:

Before our engagement the firm's owners had been 'invoicing in a vacuum' – invoicing without recourse to, or discussion with, other owners and employees. They had a typical system: Each month they distributed the WIP print-outs with time charges to each client directly to the owner responsible for invoicing each client. Each owner then drafted invoices. They were typed, reviewed by the same owner, and mailed to the clients. Owners normally did not confer with each other on how much to invoice.

We recommended that they require that any invoice with a write-down of more than five percent be approved by the managing partner, or at least by some second owner. This would allow the managing partner to discuss the value of the work with the responsible owners and perhaps help to reinforce the value of the work. The managing owner might also give them a little courage where needed to confront clients that were low in profitability.

The firm went one better; they began 'invoicing day'. Three days before the end of each month all ten owners would meet for lunch in the conference room, they would bring in sandwiches, and all owners would do their invoicing right then.

What are your current invoicing procedures for sub-standard invoices?

What mechanisms could you create in your firm to give a second owner a chance to talk the responsible owner out of a write-down?

6. Five reasons to invoice more promptly

1. WIP depreciates

2. Clients want to know what they owe

3. You get paid quicker

4. Clients remember what you did

5. *You* can remember what you did.

7. Five reasons you should invoice progressively

1. Allowing WIP to build up intimidates the accountant and increases write-downs
2. Clients would rather pay three £1,000 invoices than one £3,000 invoice
3. The larger an invoice is, the more difficult for clients to pay
4. Invoices over a certain size may require a second signature to authorise payment
5. A large invoice at the end of an engagement invites renegotiation of prices.

So break your invoices into smaller chunks.

8. Four reasons to let employees do the invoicing

Let employees draft invoices for routine work. Naturally owners should approve all invoices before sending them out. Letting employees do the invoicing has several advantages:

1. It is good training for future promotions
2. Employees are more likely to remember any extra services requested by or authorised by the client that may not have been documented in the engagement letter
3. Employees often have more courage than the owners
4. It makes the employees more cost-conscious and thus more efficient.

9. Use the invoice to sell the service

Type all invoices in your preferred office font, we suggest you default to Times Roman (the same font used in the body of this report). Do not use Initial Capitals. Courier Typefaces (Like This) Are Old Fashioned. AND ALL CAPS (LIKE THIS) ARE MORE DIFFICULT FOR PEOPLE TO READ.

- All invoices should be on letterhead.
- Use 'telephone consultation and follow-up' in preference to 'telephone call'. (This presumes there was follow-up involved with the telephone consultation.) Similarly, use 'consultation' in preference to 'discussion' or 'meeting'; and use 'research' whenever possible. This makes your services more visible and valuable to the client. Generally, the more detailed explanation you can give your clients, the better, especially regarding any potential savings or profits you have helped the client to achieve.

Example: [Description of income tax returns prepared]:

1. 'including redoing tax return for changes by client' or

2. 'including accounting for capital gains tax transactions' or

3. 'including research on dividends received from your investments'.

Generally show only one amount due for all professional services described on each invoice, with the exception of the audit fee.

Exception: When you have done extra work on a fixed-price engagement, or for a monthly-price client, show the fixed or regular price as one amount and list the extra work below with an amount for all extra work.

Here is an example of an invoice sent by one of my clients.

Example:

Regular accounting services per fixed-price agreement	750
Accounting for sale of High Street rental property	150
Accounting for sale of unit trusts under capital gains rules	175
Preparation of [description of various tax returns]	650
Amount due (before VAT)	£1,725

- Also, you can add a single line item for 'reimbursable expenses'. Reimbursable expenses should be an exact amount taken from your WIP run.
- Generally, do not invoice amounts less than £100. It causes clients to think you deal in trivia.

Industry specialities command above-average prices. Certain firms command premium prices because of their reputation for excellence in serving clients in a special industry. For example: medical practitioners, legal profession and hotels and leisure.

What existing industry specialities do you have?

How are you taking advantage of your reputation to earn above-average prices?

Bonus Point: Use higher prices during the busy season

Module 2
Avoiding write downs

Most unplanned write-downs are caused by either:

1. Estimating the engagement incorrectly (miscalculating the cost of doing the job)

Follow this procedure:

- Build a 15 percent pessimism quotient into all engagements
- The optimistic budget is only to control the job and motivate engagement team
- Give the pessimistic budget to the client.

If the client's cutoff procedures for purchases, or despatch, or invoicing, or anything else have been poor for the last several years, what makes you think they are going to be any better this year? Yet you kid yourself and budget the job assuming everything will work well. We call this the *optimistic* budget. Optimistic budgets are okay for purposes of motivating the engagement team – giving them something to shoot for. The problem arises when you use the optimistic budget to estimate the price for the client.

Even if you analyse data objectively, you learn nothing unless the data is accurate. Unfortunately, some accountants go through a rigorous process of preparing a time budget, and then neglect to post the actual time spent on the various components. Thus, they cannot compare actual to budget. The time budget does little good unless you compare it with actual. Many accountants fail to keep systematic records to track results of their budget processes. The only number they know for sure is the total hours spent by each person. But that data is available from the time reporting system and does not enable the accountant to evaluate the performance of the ones who worked on the engagement. You should treat each line item on the time budget as a contract between the firm and the personnel who are to perform that part of the engagement. If they go over budget, you need to hold them accountable. But you have to know the actual time spent on each section.

2. Not specifying clearly what is included in the price estimate and what is not (then doing extras without charging for them)

Scope creep: A phenomenon where a project creeps beyond its original scope because the client keeps asking for additional services and the accountant provides them because there are no clear boundaries.

Yet accountants often do the same thing. They quote a client a monthly retainer or a fixed price for an audit or accounting engagement without specifying clearly what the engagement includes and – more important – does *not* include.

The key to avoiding this unpleasant situation is to hold two planning conferences:
- One with the client and
- One with the engagement team who will work the engagement.

Key point: Scope creep can *only* occur with the willing consent of the accountant.

Scope creep doesn't 'just happen'. The accountant has to agree. Scope creep can come from the client's top management, but also from lower-level employees of the client who want some free help. Unfortunately, scope creep can also originate from an accounting firm employee who does 'favours' – extra free work for the client without consulting the partner.

There are two causes of scope creep: unclear project boundaries and a reluctance, unwillingness, or inability (you pick the word) within the accounting firm to stick to those boundaries.

Scope creep and small 'favours' are common in accounting practices.

3. Inefficiency (sometimes laid at the feet of the employee's supervisor)

Your firm time is an investment. When you or your employees work on a client's account you are investing your time. From this activity your clients require a return and so also does the firm. Consider this: every hour a person works has a cost to the firm. You might think of all working time (whether chargeable or non chargeable) as 'investment time'. Your people are either investing it on behalf of a client (chargeable time) or on behalf of the firm.

Here are a few ways to improve efficiency:
- Repeal *Parkinson's Law*. Employees spend so much time on engagements because of Parkinson's Law: "Work expands to fill the time available for its completion." If you give an employee an assignment without a time budget, they now have a new career. Give the employee a budget on every assignment – then hold them accountable.
- Work at the client's office. Working out of the office pays off for both owners and employees. You work more efficiently because you work straight through without interruption. If an employee needs information, he or she will find it easily from the client. In the office, the employee often leaves a message for the client and puts the file away to work on another engagement. This *put away time* and *startup time* drains efficiency.
- Exclude owner time from the budget.
- Post time backwards, with an 'hours remaining in budget'. This way the manager/senior sees a decreasing amount of time rather than an accumulating one.
- Post time daily. Have each person's time daily and compare it to budget. What gets monitored gets managed.
- Go to the client's to do your review.

Avoiding write downs

- Make sure your employees have an extras work code. One reason you do not invoice such chargeable extras is that you do not find out about them because the employees have no place to post the time. Then, make sure you bill for the extras.
- Make sure employees remuneration is based partially on how well they meet budgets.
- Bad scheduling (whoever worked the job is either over- or under-qualified) or wall-to-wall scheduling.
- Bad supervision ("Who? Me? No. But my other owners are the not performing!")

Too often accountants hide bad supervision by blaming their employees ("That employee should have done that job in 12 hours.") or bad scheduling ("If I had the right person available for that assignment, we could have made budget.") Those circumstances occur, but not as often as you pretend. When the job has gone over budget three years in a row, it is time to rethink your strategy.

Supervision is a complex issue involving, budgeting, and monitoring.

- Plan
- Budget
- Monitor

Inadequate skill in managing the client relationship; or

Lack of courage on the accountant's part (unwillingness to confront the client).

5th session

Module 3
Setting the right standard charge rates

Definition: Standard *noun*, **1** a level of quality or achievement. **2** a required or agreed level of quality or achievement. **3** something used as a measure in order to make comparisons. *adjective* **1** used or accepted as normal or average. **2** (of a size, measure, etc.) regularly used or produced. ORIGIN Old French *estendart*.
Oxford Dictionary of Current English, Third Edition

YOUR INPUT	THE CLIENT'S INTEREST IS
COST	BENEFIT
EFFORT	RESULTS
INPUT	OUTPUT
INVESTMENT	RETURN
ACTIVITIES	OUTCOMES

Your time system measures the cost, effort, and so forth that you *invest* in an engagement. But clients care principally about the right side. They care about their benefit, the results they obtain, the *value* of the service to them.

Often accountants get so caught up in their costs in the job that they lose sight of what clients really care about – value. Many professions price based on the value of the service. doctors, and dentists, for example, have fixed charges for various services they perform. For a particular service, they charge the same amount no matter how long it takes. Other professions such as insurance brokers, investment managers and estate agents price strictly on results, usually defined as a percentage of the amounts involved.

One wide-spread misconception in most accountants' thinking is that setting prices is a mathematical process based on analyses of overhead costs, salaries, competitors' charges, and so forth.

Key point: Setting prices is a marketing decision.

In fact, by actual survey, about 95% of all accountants do *not* invoice the amount their time reporting system produces. They invoice more or less than the exact figure, usually rounding the invoice (downward) to an even amount. But because the amount produced by the time reporting system influences the amount invoiced, most accountants assume the time reporting system indicates approximately the amount they *should* invoice. This is not true.

The amounts used in your time reporting system are simply the result of a management decision. You could cut those charge out rates in half, or double them, and *they would not change the value of the service* to clients.

© Marrho Limited

Setting the right standard charge out rates

Key point: Setting standard charge out rates is a management decision.

So do not confuse the *prices* you charge clients with the *standard charge out rates* you use in your time reporting system. Standard charge out rates measure *standard revenue*, or the *opportunity cost* of performing the work. They measure the *effort* the firm invested in the engagement; they do not measure the *value* of that engagement to the client.

The primary function of standard charge out rates is to serve as a rough indicator of the profitability of serving each client. You cannot over time offer a service to your clients that costs you more to provide than they are willing to pay. For example, you are capable of washing your client's windows. But if your cost of employees is more than the going rate for window washers, you cannot offer that service profitably.

Key point: The principal (and often overlooked) purpose of standard charge out rates is to determine the profitability of serving each client.

But charge out rates also represent an 'opportunity cost' to the extent that you work on clients who value your services less and who are not willing or able to pay as high a percentage of your standard time charges as other clients.

Your goal should be for all your staff to work at their highest professional level for clients that appreciate and can afford that level of service. You may only attain that level of performance 30% of the time; your employees may attain it only 50 to 70%. But that is the goal. When you achieve the goal, for most of you, that would deserve a charge out rate considerably higher than you currently use.

After all, this is the 'ideal scene' and you do not achieve that very often. But the reason most people do not achieve their goals is that they don't have any. If you keep the goal constantly in sight, it is easier to attain it.

To achieve your ideal scene, think of your charge out rates as representing the amount of value you *could* deliver to clients if all the people in your firm worked at their highest professional level, on valuable services, for clients that appreciate and can afford that level of service. Think of it as an *opportunity cost* accounting system that measures the degree to which you do not achieve your ideal scenario.

What charge out rate do you deserve when you practice at your 'ideal scenario' (the top 10% of your capabilities)?

The client evaluation process should include comparing various clients or related groups of clients in terms of the profitability of serving them. Often the demand for your services exceeds your capacity and you must decide which client to serve first or which advisory service engagement to perform. Comparing profitability of various clients allows you to make better business decisions.

Why the 2.5 percent rule is dead

Many firms use 2.5 percent (also know as the one third, one third rule) of average monthly salary for their standard charge out rate per hour. Let's see if that is appropriate. To refresh your memory: An employee earning £36,000 per year or £3,000 monthly has an hourly charge out rate of £75. If a firm wanted to generate gross sales of three times salary (£108,000 in this case), the employee must work 1,440 chargeable hours. *If* the firm also invoices 100% of standard time charges, direct salary would be 33.3% of revenues (£108,000 of revenues divided by £36,000 of salary). I noted earlier the double assumption of 1,440 chargeable hours and realisation of 100% which is the foundation of the 2.5 percent rule.

Here is the calculation:

Monthly salary	£ 3,000
	× 2.5%
Charge out rate per hour	£ 75
Assumed chargeable hours	× 1,440
Gross sales	£108,000
Assumed realisation	× 100%
Net chargeable	£108,000

Those assumptions may have had some validity in the past. Today, with increased requirements for technical education, time off, and management and marketing time, as well as an increased holiday expectation (now four/five is standard against two/three a few decades earlier) it is not always easy to yield 1,440 chargeable hours. Also, overhead costs of national insurance, PI insurance, insurance, rent, and CPD costs have risen faster than salaries. This casts doubt on the validity of the assumption that overhead equals salary cost. And most firms have a tendency to invoice at less than standard charge out rates. As a result, very few firms are getting anywhere near a three times multiple on their salary costs.

The following table calculates your actual pricing multiple.

Setting the right standard charge out rates

Line		Your firm
Salaries		
1	Professional/chargeable employees	
2	Owners	
3	[1 + 2] Total technical personnel	
4	Support personnel	
5	[3 + 4] Total salaries	£
Net fees		
6	Professional/chargeable employees	
7	Owners	
8	[6 + 7] Total technical personnel	
9	Support personnel	
10	[8 + 9] Total net fees	£
Salary multiple		
11	[6 ÷ 1] Professional employees	
12	[8 ÷ 3] Total technical personnel	
13	[10 ÷ 5] Total personnel	

What multiple of salaries does your firm generate?

Today's professional environment has increased overhead and decreased number of hours available to cover that overhead. Firms using standard charge out rates that are no longer appropriate do not earn adequate profits. If your standard charge out rates are inadequate, you should adopt a new formula. But what formula is appropriate? There are many ways to capture your costs. Here is one approach to setting appropriate standard charge out rates:

1. Determine your overhead and direct salaries (including owners' salaries)

The following table calculates your firm's overhead figures. Note that, to the extent you do not charge clients for support personnel time, those salaries are overhead for the technical employees.

Line		Your firm
	Overhead	
1	Salaries, support personnel	
2	Less, sales generated by support personnel	
3	[1 – 2] Net salaries, support personnel	
4	Other costs and expenses (All practice expenses plus interest on capital)	
5	Interest on owners' capital	
6	Personnel	
7	Facilities	
8	Practice development	
9	Other operating expenses	
10	Non-operating expenses	
11	[Sum of lines 3 – 10] Total overhead costs	
	Direct salaries	
12	Owners	
13	Professional employees	
14	[12 + 13] Total direct salaries	
15	[11 ÷ 14] Overhead as percent of direct salaries	

2. Determine an appropriate markup on your direct salaries and overhead. In other words: Decide how much sales you should be generating with your current cost structure.

Most accountants agree that the 'one-third' profit part of the 2.5 percent rule is still realistic target. That means the target markup could be viewed as fifty percent markup on the sum of direct salaries and overhead. Working with that assumption, the following table calculates the target markup and net sales for your firm's targets.

Line		Your firm
1	Direct salaries	
2	Overhead	
3	[1 + 2] Total direct costs	
4	Times markup percentage	
5	[3 x 4] Target markup	
6	[3 + 5] Targeted net sales from direct personnel	
7	Divided by realisation	
8	[6 ÷ 7] Targeted standard time charges from direct personnel	

Setting the right standard charge out rates

What markup on direct salaries and overhead is appropriate for your firm?

3. Raise standard charge out rates across the board to achieve your targets for direct personnel.

The following table calculates the average standard charge out rate increase necessary for your firm.

Line		Your firm
1	Targeted standard time charges from direct personnel	
	Direct personnel chargeable hours	
2	Owners	
3	Professional employees	
5	[2 + 3 + 5] Total	
6	[1 ÷ 5] Required average charge out rate per direct person	
7	Current standard time charges from direct personnel	
8	[7 ÷ 5] Current average charge out rate per direct person	
9	[6 ÷ 8 – 1.00] Increase necessary	

Here is another approach to calculate appropriate pricing multiples for your firm.

Line		Your firm
1	Targeted standard time charges from direct personnel	
2	Divided by direct salaries	
3	[1 ÷ 2] Annual pricing multiple	
4	Divided by utilisation for direct personnel	
5	[3 ÷ 4] Hourly pricing multiple required	
6	Divided by current pricing multiple	
7	[5 ÷ 6] Increase necessary	

How many actual chargeable hours do you currently generate per average professional employee?

What is a realistic target for average professional employee chargeable hours in the next two years? For the average owner?

Use higher rates for more valuable services

I have helped many clients analyse their standard charges into various service work codes and divide them into two types of services:

- Those which are perceived by clients to be of low value, virtually interchangeable between accounting firms, and often subject to price competition and
- Those which clients perceive as high value and, thus, less subject to price competition.

The first category are compliance services. This includes audits and accounting services such as preparing financial statements, payroll tax returns, VAT returns and similar tax forms that require no element of judgement.

The second category are advisory services. These include specialist work, niche services and your advisory services *that requires a higher level of wisdom, judgement* and expertise. These include consulting and planning services, whether personal, financial, or business. This also includes tax investigations because they require extensive negotiating skills.

Many firms find that their owners spend as little as 15 percent of their chargeable time on advisory services and almost 85 percent on compliance services. However, employees often spend very little time, maybe up to 10 percent of their chargeable time on non-compliance work with the majority being chargeable to compliance services.

We recommend a premium charge out rate for advisory services for all personnel of at least 25 percent higher than their normal rate for compliance services

The fee flexibility rule

We mentioned this earlier and here again as a reminder. Clients will generally pay up to 50% more for other non-compliance services provided they can gain the value/benefit from the service.

Module 4
Guerilla warfare

Work in progress – what should you 'invest'?

In an ideal world, no one would invest in work in progress. Every practitioner wants to convert WIP into debtors and then cash into the bank. It is a fact of life that cash in the bank starts life as WIP. Remember that we need to learn to bill clients while the tears of appreciation are still moist in their eyes? Inter firm surveys indicate that the larger the firm the more there is in WIP. I know one firm with less than 10 days in WIP and many others with 120 days or more. I have seen inter firm surveys where more than 60 firms averaged WIP of 12 percent of fees and others where the WIP has averaged more than 20 percent. One consistency in this area is the inconsistency. So, what is a fair and achievable target? If we are endeavour to bill clients promptly and avoid our WIP depreciating then a fair benchmark is six to seven weeks or around 12 percent of fees.

Your Gross Fees		£ _____
12 percent		£ _____
Your WIP	=	£ _____
Excess WIP	=	£ _____ [1]

Debtors – how much should you 'invest'?

Firstly your debtors include VAT or any other sales tax that is relevant to your jurisdiction. Inter firm surveys again highlight the inconsistency of performance. The same surveys referred to above show debtors of between 80 and 90 days with member firms ranging from 39 to 135 days with, for one association, an average of 32 days outstanding for more than 90 days. Anchoring *Defining Edge* Practice Management Strategies in being realistic, I am persuaded that there is a good case for the debtor benchmark being in the region of 22 percent of gross fees or about 80 days.

Your Gross Fees		£ _____
22 percent		£ _____
Your Debtors	=	£ _____
Excess Debtors	=	£ _____ [2]

Your total excess investment £ _____ **[1+2]**

Lock up benchmark

Dependent on your attitude and firm culture to billing, your 'investment' mix between WIP and debtors will vary. But, we can look at the overall investment in lock up. In so doing we find that my recommended investment is 34 percent, or one third, which leads me onto one rule that has evolved the more I study accountants own accounts.

The one third rule

Rule: A well managed firm should have no more than one third of its fees locked up.

What is your lock up? If your firm is greater than this, what is the adverse variance?

Interestingly, there is of course a correlation between lock up and capital required to run the business. For, again, inter firm surveys typically show that the capital required to run the 'well managed' (i.e. the practice has lock up around the one third benchmark) business is about one third of gross revenue. Now I am not saying that this is a golden rule, merely that my empirical observations lead me toward such a conclusion. However if you take out such assets as property (should they be in your balance sheet) and any attributable borrowing, what is your own capital employed? What would the owner-investment be if lock up were reduced to one third of GRF? How much external funding is standing in the place of owner capital?

If your investment in the business is greater than one third of turnover then we trust *Defining Edge* Practice Management Strategies will motivate you to take action to align your business with other well managed accountancy businesses.

In excess? Massive action campaign

Defining Edge Practice Management Strategies has already provided many insights into how to improve your firm. So, let me be clear at this point, that this next section tells the story of what I did in my own practice. I was running my practice as best I knew how. In 1988 I was privileged to be asked to speak at one of the leading USA accounting firm associations managing partner conferences. There were 40 member firms with average revenues in 1988 of $5 million. I looked at their inter firm surveys and saw what I have just described above. These were very well managed firms and much larger than my own back in Bristol. The 40 managing partners discussed lock up for over an hour; those with lower investment in lock up were grilled by those whose firms had almost become their client's bankers. Listening to these discussions I returned to Bristol determined to reduce my WIP to 10 percent. What I did I subsequently called 'guerilla billing'.

Guerilla billing

My administration manager printed off 300 cost sheets and that evening my accounts manager and I returned to the office. As we went through the files our objective was to decide a fee on account. We had some standard invoices pre-prepared with different wording for limited company accounts, unincorporated accounts and tax clients. The standard wording assured clients that this was a request payment on account and not an additional invoice. We looked at the files discussed what work had been undertaken and billed our hearts out for three hours as 220 bills stacked up on the table. The secretaries were in for a busy time.

Call and collect

You will of course recognise that I had not reduced my lock up. In fact with VAT it had, fleetingly, increased!

Before we progress onto the debtors, let me just add that for the following five years we managed to maintain our WIP at an average of between 13-15%. We had changed the culture for good.

I cannot recall the exact numbers, but it will not be a surprise to record that our debtor days increased. By the end of the 30 days after the invoices had left the office the lock up had reduced, but debtors now included at least 150 of those bills on account. We had a staff member whose responsibility it was to be responsible for chasing debts, but this largely involved standard letters followed up by phone calls which involved listening to a lot of excuses for non-payment.

It was time for action. I drafted a form called Call and Collect (sample on pg. 19). The form included 10 lines for the ten largest balances – we used the Pareto principle on the grounds that the partners could not contact everyone in one week and we wished to institutionalise the partner's involvement and responsibility for debt collection.

We worked on the basis that we called to meet with clients having come up with a reason for that meeting other than the collection of the bill. Needless to say the outstanding account was on the agenda and we found that clients were genuinely happy to pay or agree when payment would be made. We usually returned with either a cheque or standing order which normally paid the debt in three months and continued to make payments against future work.

Lock up 'nil'

If I was to look at last year's fee notes I reckon that I could probably work out 95 percent of the invoices for the next year. Certainly I believe you could perform this task in your own firm. So, let's look at a different model that results in:

1. No lock up, and

2. No partner capital to fund lock up

Agree the fee and be paid by installments. The key is to agree the whole fee (apart from any extras) and have this paid by 12 or preferably 10 equal payments. The first payment should start four months into the client accounting year and finish no later than three months after the end of the accounting year.

Call and collect					
Partner: _____ week commencing: _____					
No	Client	Balance	Called	Met	Collected
1	ABC	£5,000	Yes 10/5	28/5	Yes
2	DEF	£4,500	Yes 10/5	3/6	Post dated chqs.
3	GHI	£4,000	Yes 10/5	15/5	St. order
4	JKL	£3,500	Yes 10/5	16/55	Yes
5	ETC	£3,000	Yes 12/5	22/5	Yes
6					
7					
8					
9					
10					

Note to partner: It is your responsibility to call and meet with these clients. Calling them is not enough! Please attend to this during the week – you will receive an updated list next week. Our commitment to outstanding client service includes helping the client to make sure they pay us.

Module 5
The job is not finished until the cheque clears the bank

The previous module detailed the action I took to involve the partners and include them in the activity of debt collection. What else did I learn?

Attitude, attitude, attitude

It's all about accepting that partners have to take ultimate responsibility for collecting outstanding debts. You may not agree, but that is how I saw it then and still do today. I see debt collection as a little like factoring in that normally the debt reverts back to the company. I do believe there is a role for credit departments and for staff to call clients and ask for payment. But, to me there is no-one like the partner – this is the person the client regards as 'my accountant'.

Action, action, action

The fee should be known and accepted by the client before the bill is sent. At least that is unless the bill is more than last year's fee (still a well accepted benchmark) adjusted for inflation. From the time the invoice is sent there should be agreed procedures, allocated personnel, targets and reporting responsibilities. Whatever you do make sure that you keep up the action – even with lock up at one third that means that it takes over 120 days before payment is received. Taking that into account you may not choose to disagree with my one third rule. Good! I indicated that I was coming from a reality position, but in fact I believe that at the heart of changing the position that most accountants find themselves in is to action an approach to lock up management that is practically managed by all firm owners and utilising the relationship with clients to promote prompt payment.

Planning conference revisited

A planning conference is also intended to ensure that the clients understand what you are going to do, what you are not going to do (with special emphasis on items you did last time that you now want the client to do, or items included in the price last time that are not included now), how you will determine the price, and when the client will pay.

Include payment terms in the engagement letter

Providing for payment 'upon presentation' or 'when invoices are rendered' is not realistic for most clients and may cause them to not take your payments terms seriously. The following examples will achieve your actual collection goals and most clients will be able to accommodate these terms.

Example: Invoices will be rendered every two weeks and are payable within ten days from invoice date.

Example: All invoices are due and payable within 30 days.

Example: Our policy is to invoice every two weeks for services and costs. Payment is due by the end of the month in which invoices are rendered.

Example: We will invoice you monthly. Our invoices are payable within 15 days. Amounts outstanding at the end of the month will bear interest at ___% per annum

Sample client termination letter for non-payment of invoices

We have received no response from you to our repeated requests for payment of our invoices to you (copies attached) of £_____. Our policy is to discontinue service to any client whose account remains unpaid more than 90 days. Consequently, it is with regret that we inform you of our decision to discontinue services to you. We would like to continue our relationship with you, but we must be paid for our services.

Please be advised that all services we are currently providing you are discontinued as of this date, and no further engagements will be accepted. [OPTIONAL SENTENCE: We have requested our solicitors to take legal action to collect the outstanding debt.]

We hope you will send your cheque today so we can again render services to you in the future.

It is important to note that professional ethics may require you to ensure your client has received this letter.

Success case study

One of my sole practitioner clients with gross fees of £600,000 has no balance more than 60 days old. How do you manage to achieve this, I asked? " I train my clients to bring their cheque book with them when we meet to finalise the accounts. My invoice is on the top of their accounts box and before they leave I ask them to settle my account."

Marketing – your next generation of clients – 6th session

Module 1
Marketing – an introduction

Welcome to the sixth and final module on marketing and *Defining Edge* Practice Management Strategies.

Why leave marketing until the end?

In the twenty years plus I have been privileged to serve accountants there has been one constant with regard to feedback concerning winning new clients and that is that most new business comes from existing client referrals. Surveys show for many firms this as much as 90% of their new business. Thus the first five training sessions have provided a platform for you to assess your own performance in a range of areas. We started time together by looking at the LUBRM model identifying the keys to an accounting firm's profitability. This continued as we looked at how we deliver outstanding client service. Clients are unlikely to recommend if they are not satisfied with your service or do not consider it to be value for money. Clients tend to view *every* bill on the basis of the value they have received. If they believe you and your firm represent good value they will recommend you. People also do business with people – not just you, but your staff – everyone in the organisation will leave an impression on clients. A positive impression and they will be happy to recommend, but if clients aren't happy with the interaction with the team at your firm, they might not leave, but they may not think of recommending you either. If you scored well on the scorecard – and others agree with your rating – you have the ingredients for your clients (assuming you ask them) to be willing to recommend your services.

Extension services and cross-serving clients

Your existing clients are also candidates for your extension services. Can you identify five services that you can deliver that your clients need? It could be bookkeeping; VAT, PAYE, IT, management accounts, management meetings, estate planning, IHT planning, financial planning and so on. Have each firm owner list their top 20 clients and then across the top of the table list these five extension services. You will now have 100 service opportunities. Some will not be applicable to a particular client, others, may already have been delivered. That said, the above list of services are ones that need constant delivery or revisiting.

6th:1 Marketing – an introduction

No.	Client	1	2	3	4	5
	Service extensions – cross serving our clients					
1	ABC	D				X
2	DEF			D	D	
3	GHI	X				
4	NJK	D				X
5	MNH				D	
6	MBG			D		
7	LKI			X		
8	LPI	D				D
9	DER					
10	VGY		D			
11	HGF		X	D		D
12	YYT					
13	KJH	X		X		X
14	OIU			X		
15	BNM		D			D
16	YTR	X				v
17	RFB			X	X	
18	MFW					
19	VGH		D	X		
20	BHJ					

Key

1-5: Your extension services (see page 1)

D: Service already delivered

X: Service not appropriate

Note: the blanks represent service opportunities – over a two to three year time period seek opportunity to see which of your clients are interested in these service extensions

While there is no doubt business to be retained, referrals from clients and extension services there are also new clients to be won through marketing.

There are many books that have been written on the subject of marketing as well as many seminars. My approach in this last series of modules is to provide some good solid theory and then to suggest a series of marketing strategies and tactics to blend into your firm's marketing programme.

Marketing is not an activity that can be isolated or independent of other practice drivers. Marketing should be developed in context of the firm, its objectives, the objectives of the owners and the needs of clients. Thus the role of marketing must be integral to the firm's strategic planning.

If the firm is 'small' and intending to remain so then the required results from marketing will be determined by the owner(s). With an ever-increasing regulatory regime that involves deadlines, fines and penalties a sole practitioner, or even two-three partner firm may not wish to increase in size. Gross fees may increase steadily with clients lost by attrition replaced through referrals from clients and professional referrals. Ownership may not wish to grow at more than, say three to five percent a year. More specifically ownership may not wish to grow the firm's total hours output.

Does marketing have a role to play in this situation? Yes, but the marketing activities will be influenced by ownership's agenda.

If the firm is medium-sized and seeking to maintain market share then the marketing activities are likely to involve the owners as marketers accompanied by some form of marketing programme that may be overseen by the partners (although not someone called a marketing partner!), administrative staff or possibly the marketing programme is partly overseen by a Marketing Director. Some firms that have gross fees of between £250,000 and £1 million may have a staff member involved with marketing on a part-time or full time basis. Others may engage an external marketing consultant who may or may not be 'hands-on'.

If the firm has fees in excess of £1 million it is likely that some, but not necessarily all, of the owners, will have thus far played a key role in winning new business. However, the larger the business the greater the need for replacing clients and the internal clamour for 'new clients'. Larger firms will almost certainly have a marketing function that is more evidently 'armoured' than is perhaps the case with small or medium-sized firms. With client losses year-on-year probably in the region of seven percent the need for new business is more acute and hence marketing is an accepted activity with its own budget, its own allocation of human resource and reporting structure. The institutionalisation of the marketing programme may appear to transfer the weight of responsibility away from the partners whereas in reality there is a greater need for owners to be involved in order to support the marketing investment. Thus partners assume a role that extends to include activities such as networking and sales.

Not necessarily, but maybe you can identify where in your firm marketing fits and how marketing needs to serve the firm in the future. Let's ask ourselves:

- What are we marketing?
- What is the service?
- What is the value proposition?
- What are the tangible benefits?
- What are the emotional benefits?
- What is the cost?

Marketing needs resourcing and two of the key constituent components are financial and human resources. Financially, I believe that once a firm grosses above £1 million a funding requirement of 3 percent of gross income is appropriate and necessary. Below that level 2 percent is my recommended minimum. What do firms spend? Given that marketing can appear on a number of lines in the profit and loss account (postage, stationery, advertising, website, entertaining, etc) it is not always easy to interpret the results from inter firm surveys. However, expenditure is normally 1.5 percent, or less.

The second resource requirement is time. Setting side the question of marketing staff time the marketing activity requires the time of firm owners. In my view, regardless of firm size owners should commit a minimum of 200 hours a year to marketing.

A selection of training topics for marketers

I was for many years a member of the Association of Accounting Marketers based in Kansas, USA. This association has members who I regard at the top end of their profession. I was privileged to attend their conferences and meet some of their members who were so totally committed to the cause of marketing the accounting firm. Most of them were marketing professionals who had trained in the disciple of marketing

A selection of the training topics from the Association of Accounting Marketers Conferences:

- Open your mind for revolutionary marketing
- Promoting partner performance
- Managing your sales team: your partners and your staff
- The power of publicity
- Creating rainmakers
- Branding from the inside out
- Overcoming the partner/marketer disconnect
- A revolutionary approach to developing a sales culture
- Sales secrets your firm can't live without
- 10 management practices that can make or break a marketing plan
- Effective employee incentive programmes
- Seven key reasons sales are lost and what to do about it
- How professional service firms compete to win
- Women who mean business: Playing to win
- Multi offices marketing and sales
- How to transfer accountants into effective business generators

The Association of Accounting Marketing holds an annual conference. Over the years it was one of the best conferences I had the privilege of attending. To learn more visit: www.accountingmarketing.org/

My thanks to all those members of AAM who became my friends.

Module 2
Marketing planning

We have discussed in earlier training sessions the essential strategies that comprise the elements to enable a firm to deliver outstanding client service. As night follows day a firm that delivers outstanding client service will have a good reputation among clients that will lead:

- to an increase in referrals, that will lead
- to an increase in new clients, that will lead
- to an enhanced reputation in the community

How can a firm grow and win business beyond those afforded by client referrals?

Planning to gain new clients

Some firms manage themselves without any formal planning process. That's not to say there are no plans it's just that these are not formalised, so they may reside in the mind of one or more individuals, and others will generally be in the dark. In this situation, firm members' role is to work without a clearly defined understanding of the firm's plans. They may hear snippets of information, they may make certain assumptions and draw certain conclusions, but the big picture and how they fit into it is not necessarily clear. They may 'hear' about the plans, but they are not sure if or when these plans will come to pass.

The plan should be communicated to everyone in the firm and made available on the firm's network, possibly in an 'executive summary' format.

The advantage of this strategy is that in order to develop the plan, management must commit to the planning process, consider the firm's mission and take a look at how the future might transpire and what has to be done to enable the firm and its staff to realise their full potential in seeking to meet the needs of their clients.

Thus, what we have described in *Defining Edge* Practice Management Strategies so far, we regard as the bare necessities for a successful an accounting practice. Alternatively, you could view our journey thus far as insights into best practice upon which you have your own views and you will with each of the activities we describe either agree or agree to disagree and be able to decide the extent to which you could improve in each of these areas.

Become convinced and captivated by planning and you will become an advocate for planning, not only for yourself and your firm **but also with clients**, which does of course provide a service delivery opportunity that you can personally vouch for as a necessity. You owe it to yourself, your co-owners and team members to be the best you can be. You owe it to clients to be the best accountant/adviser knowing that the community needs the value you bring to the marketplace. Put more succinctly, if you do not meet and exceed the expectations of the clients – someone else might take your place.

Steps in the marketing planning process

Firm owners need to take a wider look at the firm's business plan as this will provide the strategies to be addressed in the firm's strategic marketing plan. The firm's business plan impacts the development of the strategic marketing plan in areas such as desired growth and service development. My advice now for the marketing planning is written as though you are the firm's marketing director.

The next eight pages adopt an approach to planning for firms that are committed to marketing and have fee income in excess of two million pounds. If your revenue is less than that, tailor the planning approaches that you consider appropriate.

What is strategic marketing planning?

You need a clear understanding of who you are and what the firm is capable of, what business you are in, the value you create for your clients, and how you differentiate yourselves in winning and retaining clients. The key is to create the means to make the most of whatever your business environment presents. The task for owners is to create strategic thinking and develop strategic plans to create success.

Leadership is important

In the process of developing a plan, answers come through a careful process of creative thinking and logical reasoning that must be unique to your firm. The process of strategic planning or goal setting has fundamental features that make it relevant to almost *any* challenge facing *any* accounting firm. But leadership is vital to achieve success. Someone needs to put the right people in the right places and build a 'marketing culture' and a marketing team. Someone has to build consensus about the plan, communicate it widely and reinforce it frequently, and at least one individual needs to face difficult issues and make tough decisions.

Designing a strategy – how not to do it

There are those accounting firms that have a planning system that is bottom heavy. They spend a great deal of time getting all of those involved in client service, departmental and individual tactical plans in place, but little or no time thinking about the basic strategy or direction of the business. To correct this approach, some firms try to set firmwide goals, which can include tactics that involve the whole firm, such as starting a client satisfaction survey, or starting a marketing training programme for staff, or sending out regular press releases. These are examples of marketing tactics. Firms must go through the planning process before they begin doing these. Some firms create grandiose strategic plans, supported by elaborate detailed budgets, resource estimates, tactical plans and timetables, most of which ultimately have little connectivity to the success of the business.

Designing a strategy – how to do it

Think about the future. What services do your clients need? Where does your firm want to be in the next three to five years? Focus on 'futuring' as an integral element of your planning. Futuring should be used to form a picture of the direction in which you need to head. Be prepared to ask the tough questions such as: Is our tax return service becoming obsolete? Should we still focus on processing of tax returns? What will our staff do between 1 December (will this eventually be 1 October?) and 5 April? Should we use paraprofessionals? Should we hire staff on tax season contracts? Should we train our staff to focus on other growing/emerging areas of practice such as business valuations; technology consulting; HR consulting; estate planning; retirement planning and so on. While developing a plan is necessary, it should focus on the 'future' picture and how that picture will be drawn and completed?

The six levels of strategic planning success

1. Vision

Who is (your firm) and what do we want to become?

2. Mission statement

It is helpful to create a written statement of how the firm must do business, how you define clients, what value you create for clients, how to retain their business, and how you can work with clients to gain constructive feedback regarding their needs and desires and your performance. Many firms come up with a document to serve as a strategy statement, a statement of philosophy, a value statement, or a company policy, but too often even the most basic document never seems to be finalised and broadcast. Your mission statement should go beyond the 'word smithing' to form an image of the firm. Someone who is reading it should be able to ascertain the qualities that make you unique relative to other firms. Your statement should be short, memorable and easy to remember.

3. External information about the market – opportunities and threats

You need some indication about what is going on in the marketplace outside your office with your competitors, the national and local economy, considering technology advances, changes in demographics all within your defined geographic market.

4. Internal strengths and weaknesses

Work with your team to obtain their perspectives about the firm. Ask questions including, Who are we? What are we good at? Are we a team? What are we committed to? What are our best opportunities? How good are we at accommodating to and managing change?

5. Goals for growth

These can include both qualitative such as 'we want to become the number one medical practitioners accounting firm in...', or quantitative goals, including fee/growth targets, market share targets and so on. It is important that these goals be as realistic and specific as possible, and be supported with a detailed tactical plan.

6. Implementation and measurement

Don't keep your plan a secret. Set realistic targets, provide training to individuals who are responsible for implementation, keep the strategic marketing plan as simple as possible, and try to make it measurable.

The purpose of a strategic marketing plan

There are a variety of factors in today's challenging business environment that make practice development and marketing efforts vital to any accounting firm, not only as a means of expansion, but also to preserve the firm's existing fee base.

Survival

Any professional practice understands that clients cease to require service for a range of valid and acceptable reasons...companies expand, merge, relocate, cease to trade. Somewhere in the region of seven percent of fees are lost annually through attrition. To stay at the same level of fee income, at the very least, you must replace these 'natural' losses, whatever their cause and continue to provide outstanding client service.

Competition

The marketplace continues to increase in competitiveness. There are more accountants than ever including those who are 'non-qualified'. That is not surprising given that accountancy continues to be a high margin business and open to all. Accountants are devoting 15% more hours to marketing than ever before...all of which makes for a highly competitive marketplace. To effectively compete, accountants have to develop and market unique selling features, which are not available elsewhere and must substantiate fees by emphasising the value the firm provides.

Change

Your firm has to date been successful. You have made it through the first part of the 21st century, years in which there were a reduced number of companies requiring audits and a trend toward filing everything online with ever tighter filing timetables. During these years there has been a clear change in the philosophy of the marketplace as the mystique of the accountant has been rolled back and there is now a clearer picture of what goes on in the accountant's 'black tent'. Many clients are looking to do more for themselves but still expect more from the accountant who is now so engaged in some of the more routine accounting work. Some practices have defaulted to looking for more clients to fill the compliance service pipeline while others have expanded their service portfolio and become more consultative. Many clients expect us to help them avoid accounting problems rather than solve them and many types of accounting and tax return work have become commodities in the marketplace. Generally, clients now have higher expectations in areas such as timeliness, value and service.

The big picture

By taking a big picture view of marketing and by placing the client at the centre of that picture, you come to realise that marketing is a means of survival as well as a path to an increase in prosperity. Do not forget that your strategic marketing plan must have the client at the centre. This does of course include existing and prospective clients.

Fulfilment

The purpose of strategic planning and developing an ongoing marketing programme is to improve the flow of quality clients into the firm and increase client satisfaction with the firm's services. However, marketing should also fulfill the needs of the firm's team members to work at a firm they regard as successful and a valuable member of the community and the profession. Marketing is not advertising, or telemarketing, but a continuing sophisticated combination of ascertaining the ongoing accounting tax and advisory needs of target groups and organising people and services to meet those needs in an outstanding manner at an appropriate level of profit.

The future

An equally important aspect of marketing is looking into the future to consider what services clients will require. Your strategic marketing plan needs to identify what evolving services will be required in the next three to five years, and move in the direction of capitalising on these opportunities. At the same time, your firm should also be aware of any areas of service for which there is a reduced demand.

Clear direction and control

A good strategic marketing plan can provide control and direction, as you maintain and increase the growth of the firm. Your plan should detail growth objectives and the strategies and actions required to achieve those objectives. The implementation of the actions will result in a stronger, healthier, and more profitable practice that better meets the client needs'.

Where to begin

Step 1: Situation analysis and meetings with key individuals

You will need to convene a meeting with key individuals including firm owners and any other team managers/directors who are interested and/or involved in the firm's marketing programme.

You will also need to review the firm's existing marketing ambassadors and determine how members of the firm are utilising these resources.

Step 2: Vision session or retreat

It can be helpful to this process to have either a half day retreat or a 'vision' session in the office. In larger firms, it may be necessary to hold a series of vision meetings. The purpose of the retreat or vision meetings is to gather information from within the firm and build consensus and commitment among the group. It may be a good idea to perform a SWOT analysis. These meetings should be facilitated by an individual who can work toward assisting everyone focus on the perceived position of the firm in the marketplace and in the mind of clients; assessing the firm's potential; target growth plans and opportunities to gain new business, including services to existing clients and services to new clients.

Planning a marketing retreat or vision session

First, identify your goals and give all participants an agenda that enables them to understand the purpose of the meeting and their pre-meeting actions and contribution required during the meeting.

Your goals are to:
- Encourage open discussion
- Solicit ideas from everyone in the group
- Build consensus
- Encourage out-of-the box thinking
- Ask the tough questions
- Formulate conclusions at each meeting
- Cut short any discussion that is critical of an individual
- Cut off discussion that is going down a blind alley
- Have fun
- Provide a written plan for follow up.

At the meeting

Start by asking everyone to clarify their expectations for the outcome of the meeting

Then take time out to setting the meeting in context

- How has our business changed over the last year? Three years?
- What changes do we see in the next three to one to five years?
- What are the primary drivers for these changes?
- From our past experiences, how have we adapted to the changes in the last three years – lessons learned?

- What has given us the ability to successfully adapt?
- How would you describe our marketing culture?
- What are our key strengths and our weaknesses?
- How does the firm differ from our competitors?
- Why do clients use our firm?
- How do we feel about our performance standards and work quality?

Other areas you may cover include:

- Personal relationships
- Niche skills
- Knowledge of client industry/business
- Written/verbal communication skills
- Professional image/reputation
- Location
- Fees
- Dependability and reliability
- Availability
- Profitability

Now, looking forward

- Where do we want to be in three to five years?
- What suggestions/strategies do you have for achieving growth?
- What are our major opportunities and threats?

Develop shared goals and a unified approach

Prepare an executive summary of your meeting

List your target client types

Identify three priorities to accomplish over the next three months and ten priorities over the next 10 months

Finally

- Create a draft, strategic marketing plan as a discussion document for firm owners including:

- Identify your goals, e.g. grow the tax practice by 10 percent; win two audits...
- List the strategies planned to achieve goals, e.g update website for new medical practitioner's service group; set up a client team for medical practitioners; develop a letter to clients on estate planning.
- Set priorities
- Budget
- Develop a detailed marketing calendar
- Implement, monitor, fine-tune plan
- Measure results
- Broadcast:
    - Successes
    - Next three key marketing activities

Step 3. Client feedback

During this process do not overlook the importance of client feedback. Select, a cross section of, say, 10 clients for interview to evaluate their view of the firm. It is preferable to conduct meetings face-to-face, but mailed surveys work if the client is called in advance, and also thanked. Let your client know he is one of an elite group being asked for feedback- and thank them when they have completed the interview or survey – maybe a two or six bottle case of quality wine.

Step 4. Market research

Information about the marketplace is essential and this information is readily available from agencies such as D&B, ICC, Jordans and so on. These agencies are able to provide mailing lists that can augment your own mailing list. As ever, no mailing list can be imported without screening and deduping.

Step 5. Multi level planning

Strategic marketing plan

The final step in the strategic marketing planning process is the development of a written plan. Make the plan concise, possibly no more then five pages in length – and make the first page an executive summary. The appendix to the plan will detail the plans for areas such as client relations; team member activities; plans to update the website; development of firm ambassadors; any advertising that is planned; public relations programme, as well as a comprehensive 'action items' list, implementation schedule and marketing budget. The plan will contain defined goals and targets, as well as key result areas, which should be realistic and measurable.

Practice specialisms or niche area strategic marketing plan

You may also find it appropriate and necessary to develop a strategic marketing plan for your specific practice groups, niche areas of practice, or even individual clients. Follow the structure in your firm's marketing strategic plan in order to facilitate consistency in style and ensure that these plans are again goal oriented and concise.

Personal marketing plans (PMP)

Every firm owner and possibly the managers should have a PMP. On the basis that (some) managers aspire to firm ownership they should be involved with marketing as the ability to win new business should be one of the conditions for future participation in firm ownership.

The PMP is valuable for four reasons:

1. It helps the individual articulate their goals and become committed to their role in marketing

2. It helps you manage your referral programme so that firm owners have firm-strategic relationships

3. It provides you with a way to assign marketing budgets to individuals

4. Everyone who has a PMP will have prospects.

Five market segments

There are five primary market segments in which marketing should be directed. These should be reflected in your marketing plan(s).

1. Members of the firm

This includes all team members. All team members have a responsibility to market the firm and they should be empowered to do so. Make sure everyone is aware of the firm's capabilities and expertise, and involve as many of the team as you can in client relations and business development.

2. Firm owners

There is no excuse for a firm owner to devote less than 200 hours to marketing. If the owner is a founder there will be no need to remind them of the importance of marketing. However, second generation owners are not always as committed to marketing. There are many reasons for this not least the fact that society today has different ethics, rules and values and owners do not all wish to work 50 or more hours a week.

3. Existing clients

Existing clients should be your best source of referrals. As night follows day, provide outstanding client service and you will gain referrals. Outstanding client service includes cross serving clients with your *advisory and extension services* in addition to your *compliance services*. Probably, a large proportion of your clients are unaware of the full range of your services. It is essential to analyse the needs, expectations and desires of your clients and then develop your marketing and client interactions to offer these services to clients.

4. Prospect clients

These include clients that the firm does not currently work with but has a high desire to add these clients to the firm's client portfolio. Typically a firm should have a prospect list. How many? My advice is that the prospect list should not be too long. I recommend that the firm has a base prospect list of 50 firms increased by 50 for every firm owner. Calculate the total and half it by all means, do not however double it! Be targeted, both in terms of industry, geographic location and size of client.

5. Referral sources

Make sure that each firm owner has at least six referrals. Meet with them, send them multiple copies of marketing literature (How many? Start with three). Send them clients, get to know them, socialise, but above all deliver outstanding service to their referrals.

Module 3
Core marketing strategies

Let's look in further detail at some key components in your marketing proposition.

We have already examined some of the key management components that comprise the foundation stones of a successful marketing plan. Thus far we have endeavoured to describe such areas as client need, firm services, personal development and discuss levels of attainment in each area. We have discussed how a high commitment to delivering outstanding service will enable you to sell more hours, win new clients and gain a high level reputation for quality work.

Q: So, is this the module we start to look specifically at marketing?

A: Well, yes, but probably not how you would suspect, at least not yet. The reason for this is that we wish to demonstrate how much of marketing should emanate from outstanding client service. In other words we are looking at marketing, but from an alternative perspective. That is one which compels action because it is clearly something that should be done as opposed to these are some ideas from a marketing seminar which I may, or may not consider at some point of time in the future. At this point we look at strategies that may be used with clients (marketing to clients is an important aspect of marketing and client care) and referrals and prospects.

Let's look at some of these (in alphabetical order):

1. Advisory literature

Research into the effectiveness of communication suggests that as little of seven per cent of what is said is accurately heard and remembered. In fact research suggests that eight percent of what people recall from initial meetings was never said. Verbal communication is not as effective a means of communicating information as we might think and it is possible that we are not always the outstanding communicators we think we are. What is the effective charge rate per hour when only just over four minutes are remembered? The point here is that it is important to recognise that outstanding client service includes giving clients options for assimilating information and advice. Information, albeit standard text or edited tailored text gives the client the opportunity to consider this in the client's own time and rate of learning. Providing the client with information may also enable them to decide themselves what course of action to take while on the other hand they may have questions to ask as a result of what they read.

Marketing point: Include a summary and samples of your range of literature in reception for visitors to view and take away. Provide your referrals sources with samples that they can hand out to their clients.

Ambassadors

As part of your outstanding client service and marketing commitment you should commit to a *client-care communication campaign (4Cs)*.

There are a number of reasons why you should have a 4c programme, including:

- the opportunity to remind your clients regarding your interest in them as clients – maybe a personal note could be appended to client letters
- the opportunity to highlight areas that you know are likely to be of interest to clients, e.g. succession, trusts, tax minimisation, tax changes, IHT, retirement and so on
- you could enclose a spare copy of the publication for the client to pass on to a business colleague
- your 4Cs programme reminds the client that they are with an up-to-date and proactive adviser
- your 4C programme gives you the chance to let clients know what they need to know re compliance matters, e.g. key dates and deadlines
- the opportunity of firm news updates including staff and new services

Your 4Cs programme could include publications such as:

- A tax strategies brochure
- A Budget report
- A tax card
- Client newsletter
- Client update or mini-guide

Your 4Cs programme and the internet

Do you collect client email addresses? Many firms now send weekly or monthly news updates using a mail cannon. Currently the most popular and widely used format is html.

Possible objections

1. It's too expensive:

In an industry that has such high margins and so historical a service that is so closely associated with tax liabilities, surely you cannot afford not to invest in giving clients the opportunity to look at their future – your 4Cs programme is your chance to position yourself as part of their planning process.

2. Client's don't want newsletters or...

Firstly, where are your ambassadors on the quality scale. If not a 9 or 10 (on a scale of 1 to 10 where 10 is outstanding), then what do you need to do to improve the quality? Is your view based on more than just a few client comments? Remember that any client mailshot should include a bounce-back process that provides clients with the opportunity to say, thanks but no more please. The bounce back should also give opportunity for clients to ask for more information/help.

2. Car park

Do you have spaces reserved for clients, referrals and other visitors to your office? Is the car park clean and weed free?

Marketing point: With many offices in areas where parking is difficult and often costly, anything you can do to improve the client's journey will reduce the 'irritation' factor. Small point but this assists in deterring new clients from 'making the effort' to visit the office. If you are 'stuck' with a problem in this area – stress your willingness to travel and meet clients – an approach which may well be appropriate regardless of parking facilities.

3. Owners

It's your business – if you are not the founder then someone before you entrepreneured and grew the firm you now have an ownership in. Marketing is not a **CPD** activity it is a **MYOB** (mind your own business) activity. Your personal marketing programme should, no let's make that must, include:

- being a marketing leader
- meeting with clients and asking at least 75% if they know anyone else who needs "a great accountant" or an accountant who knows how to reduce tax, or ".........."
- meeting at least bi-annually with a minimum of six referrals
- investing a minimum of 200 hours per annum on marketing
- fully supporting the firm's marketing calendar and activities and making yourself available when marketing activities are being held.

4. Personnel

All firm team members, have a responsibility to broadcast the firm and its services. Let us look at what will assist staff in this area:

Training – internally to start with, maybe looking for cross-serving opportunities within the client base. Can they add names to the firm's database of prospects? Who do they know who should be a client? What clubs or associations do they belong to? How are they (or could they be) involved with the community?

Rewarding – "its's part of their job to introduce clients to the firm"

"Yes, but do they and if they do are we maximising this source of new business?"

"Well we've started a reward scheme in the past and we never seemed to pay anything out, so we think that this does not work. In fact we know it doesn't work".

"Hhhhhhm. Well, I understand and have myself also known firms that have tried to reward staff for introducing clients to the firm and they too have reported that it was like "pulling teeth". However, this is an area that we revisit because:

- winning clients through leads from staff is the ultimate reward for having a firm-wide marketing culture and commitment
- staff should have the opportunity of being motivated to win business for the firm- after all the firm needs clients to provide everyone their livelihood
- there is a need to train the next generation of firm owners in how to win new business – just in case anyone should think that the firm has a divine right to new clients, or that new clients "walk in through the front door like gravity causes an apple to fall to the ground".

Two schemes that work:

- The ten percent scheme
- The marketing miles scheme

Empowering – train, encourage, involve, set goals for activities not results

Enabling – give them a time budget, an unlimited cash budget (what's the most they will spend?). Agree with them their activities, type and frequency.

5. Reception

First impressions are lasting impressions. Go into a department store and you expect to find this well lit, well laid out with a range of attractive goods for sale. Somewhere ahead of you there is a store guide that gives an overview of all the various goods you will find on all the stores floors. Enter the reception of a major firm of lawyers in London and you will probably look around at the expensive and expansive furniture, the artwork as well as *both* the receptionists. Yes, the size and quality of reception experience creates an impression that registers a note on the expectancy chord – "this is a firm that is going to give good advice – and yes, it will cost!"

What *wow* factor does your reception give?

A few pointers:

Have you invested in reception and your reception rooms? Well *decorated* with good *quality furniture* and good *quality* (possibly local) *artwork*?

Am I going to receive a *warm and personal welcome* from the receptionist – maybe the receptionist has a record of how I like my tea/coffee?

Visiting reception – a 'case study'

Before I sit down, I notice a number of *attractive certificates* which remind me of the number of networks and associations my accountants are members of, they look good, in fact I am pleased to see that they are so well connected and up-to-date. As I sit down in reception (knowing that it will be five minutes before Blake appears for our meeting I am able to decide if I should read the local or national paper. Alternatively, I see that I am able to pick up a couple of copies of the last two *newsletters* together with a couple of *tax cards* and a comprehensive list of the firm's *advisory literature*. Now, what's this? A *menu of services* including some of the benefits of a Financial Planning Review; Business Planning Service; Estate Planning Review; Management Accounts; IT Systems installation; book keeping advice; payroll; HR services – and that's in addition to the service they already provide!

Blake says to himself, "I really didn't know my accountants offered some of those services – I was thinking of going to my solicitors' to look at my Will; my IFA for an estate review and my computer supplier to discuss a new system for the company – looks like *I* need to *ask* Blake about some of *his* firm's services! This menu of services has been really useful!

"Now, do I have time to *check my inbox* for mail – it's so useful knowing that I can access the internet when I come here."

"Is everything alright with you and the family? How was your holiday to France?"

"Sally and I spoke a few months ago about our plans for the holidays – that was kind of her to remember. I recall last time I was here she smiled and asked me if I would mind completing a client survey – didn't take long – just a few questions asking for some routine feedback on the firm's services – I liked the one they slipped in at the end asking me if I knew anyone else who would benefit from their services – I don't think about my accountants very often but I was happy to suggest a couple of my friends who I know would benefit from having better accountants.

"Ah, Blake is here and I know that Sally is going to take my coffee through to the meeting room. I used to meet in Blake's office where I could see all the files he was working on around the floor. The new meeting rooms are a great improvement, Blake and I are able to access the internet and he is able to show me my accounts using PowerPoint – I particularly find his use of excel spinners helpful."

Any lessons you can apply from the case study?

6. Referrals

There are two principal referral sources:

1. Professionals

2. All others – we prefer to call these referrers 'advocates'. This group includes friends, family and clients.

Key point: In order to provide an outstanding service to clients an accountant should be able to refer a client to two bankers, two IFAs, and two solicitors.

What is your referral contact programme?

7. Seminars

Seminars provide an opportunity to showcase the compass of your abilities. Firms that have an annual programme of 2-8 or more seminars a year attest to the value of seminars as a way to 'broadcast' to clients regarding planning issues. For example clients associate accountants with tax minimisation, and there are opportunities to present planning strategies and solutions. Seminars also provide a framework for working with referrals such as banks and IFAs and providing a variety of speakers from disciplines other than accountancy. These speakers should come from firms you are happy to be associated with and hopefully referrals are already passing between any firms with whom you associate.

Marketing point: Seminars are occasions when you can invite your prospects. Those who are warm prospects can see how you compare with their current accountant '. If your referrals are present this indicates their 'approval' of your firm.

8. Souvenirs

Do your financial statements look the same as every other firms? How 'unknown' is the information contained therein? On a referrals' desk would the financial statements appear impressive?

Marketing point: Extending the content of the financial statements (and the Tax Return), gives greater value, improves retention as well as impressing your customers who may see the reports, e.g. bank managers.

9. Stationery

Make sure your stationery, including envelopes, report covers, accounting statements and so on are well designed and on a good quality paper stock.

10. Technology

Technology continues to offer ever-innovative ways of marketing. Here is a selection of the technology routes that some use to promote themselves and their firms:

RSS feeds – Really simple syndication – is a way of distributing content to users without them ever having to come to your website. This is particularly useful for those firms who are creating regular new content.

To use an RSS News Feed your user need to have a News Reader, a piece of software that allows you to subscribe to RSS Feeds and view from a browser or desktop e.g. http://www.bloglines.com

The user will now be collating regularly updated headlines from their favourite content sites.

This will mean you are communicating to your market and enhancing the chances of the content being seen, and more importantly read and responded to. As RSS Feeds run on categories you can set up a set of general or very sector-specific feeds for your users to subscribe to. Owners could consider RSS Feeds as an excellent way for to gather intelligence on and stay a breast of things which may affect their key markets. Setting up an RSS Feed from your website site should be relatively straight forward.

Social networking – e.g. LinkedIn, Facebook – social networking does have an important business face, and should not be dismissed without some careful thought.

People do business with people, and like it or not the ability to maintain an important web profile has never been as easy or as important. Handled well and with careful thought an impressive and mature Facebook entry can make a welcome link from your website, and also provide a useful signpost back to your site.

LinkedIn, the business end of social networking, has established a strong world wide reputation and you may feel more comfortable with a provider which positions it as such. Owner profiles with links to Linkedin entries can look progressive and interesting as well as serving to increase their own personal brand. Social networks can also provide excellent resources for research, lead generation, and market intelligence.

Search engine optimisation (SEO) – SEO has been popular since the commercial benefits of Internet searching were recognised. Being found is now seen as essential for websites that are competing for attention. Search should not be seen as an exercise that can be carried out once and without any bearing on your other activities. SEO is in fact a process and a discipline that can, if effectively applied, be very rewarding.

Much SEO is achievable through understanding and executing some basic principles that require little or no technical skill (easy access to your sites content through a Content Management System is highly preferable), however a good SEO consultant can be worth their weight in gold. SEO can be a complex, daunting and time consuming area, although the basic principles are easy to learn and understand. This is why a decision needs to be made about how important it is to your overall marketing activity.

Pay per click advertising (PPC) – Search engines return results for specific searches and include sponsored links to relevant sites. The owners of these adverts are only charged when their ad is actually clicked on. This mechanism is called Pay Per Click. PPC has grown in popularity over the last few years.

Some thought that professional service companies did not easily lend themselves to PPC campaigns, as the services offered are less transactional and more relationship based. In reality this is not how users now see things. Users react to the best response to their search request and if this happens to be a sponsored link then that is certainly one they will visit. The costs can be very small as search volumes for accountancy are much fewer compared to consumer markets.

All the major search engines have their own easy to use PPC programs that you can use such as http://adwords.google.com.

The key here is to also think about short, punchy and compelling messages, strong call to actions and creating specific landing pages.

Blogs – Web Logs, or Blogs are online journals which can be used in a variety of business contexts to show depth of experience, provide or provoke opinion and debate, and create insights into topical issues which can be harnessed to increase your firms presence and reputation. Blogs are most frequently centred on a person within the firm rather than the firm itself – this permits a much more personal and frank dialogue rather than a more even handed and neutral corporate communication.

Because they are so personal they are often more highly charged than other forms of marketing, so it is usually advisable to provide the final editorial brush to any new posting. Even more key is actually finding the best person to do it. Which often means those that have the time, energy and commitment to provide regular postings. A well written Blog can create a real differentiator between you and your competitors.

Email marketing – The principles of direct marketing are quite mature now, as are the data protection laws guiding it. Legislation and technology now combine to try and provide not just protection for consumers but also guidelines that create focus and opportunities for marketers.

Professional service marketers these days use email in more subtle ways to engage targeted groups with information and content that will aid and inform them, even on an individual basis. It can be used along with subscription or registration processes to create permission-based distribution lists, or even informal networking devices.

However the real power of email marketing comes from driving traffic to specific pages on your website – regular emailed newsletters are great devices to do this. There are also programs that will allow you to track exactly who clicked what links to view which pages. This kind of data is invaluable to building up an understanding of where your opportunities lie.

Web statistics – No matter what marketing you engage in there is always pressure to look at the ROI. Being armed with site statistics is an excellent way of reporting the value of your site providing that the metrics are benchmarked or analysed in context of overall lead or fee performance. In the last few years some excellent products have become available. Most notably though Google Analytics http://www.google.com/analytics/ which provides powerful insights into the activity of users in the typically easy-to-use way for which Google is renowned. Such powerful tools not only allow for great reporting they can also be used to aid the planning and finessing of your website into a truly powerful online presence.

11. Website

Probably more than 90% of your clients, prospects and referrals are accustomed to being able accessing the three billion plus websites accessible on the internet. Is your site one that impresses? Is it up-to-date? Do you provide online services? Can clients access their documents in a client secure area?

Here are some of the content areas that I believe should be on a good accountants website:

These areas and functionality include:

Home page

Avoid including more than 100 words in your introductory text, but do include links within the site.

About us

- Include images of firm owners (graphics/cartoons if you prefer)
- Include a brief owner bio, maybe a note regarding personal interests/hobbies
- Include email address

Our services

Street surveys reveal that most people cannot list more than two services offered by accountants. Prepare your descriptions and focus on the benefits rather than features. Inclusion of case studies and testimonials provides a powerful dimension to your service offering. Refer to the individuals who provide a particular service and include an email link.

Contact us

Include your address, location directions, maybe an image of your office and possibly a link to Google maps.

Links

Sites should provide clients with a major portal to the internet and include links to hundreds of 'essential' websites.

Online services

These might include company formation and access to information reports.

Client only area

Provide your clients with a personal online area where they can access a selection of their own documents and so on.

Site information content

Visit the providers of hosted website content services for ideas on content – these managed sites include content on business, personal and tax planning matters.

Calculators

As well as the ones that clients would expect such as PAYE; VAT; car/van benefit; loan and stamp duty calculators. Some sites include others such as car cost; savings and millionaire calculators.

A reminder

This module highlights some of the key marketing activities to institutionalise in the firm. Does the above list constitute marketing?

Rather than answer that question directly, it is perhaps more appropriate to point out that these are activities to include in your marketing. As such they demonstrate that marketing cannot be seen in isolation to the firm's management or client service commitment. I also seek to demonstrate the principal that so much of what is regarded as marketing is in fact a necessary activity for the delivery of outstanding client service.

Module 4
Reputation and relationships

We have already suggested firm owners should engage with the marketing activity for a minimum of 200 hours a year – about four hours a week. This module provides over 40 activities, all of which could be the responsibility of owners. It is important to enjoy marketing so look through these activities and see which ones will work for you and coincide with the firm's marketing plan. The first section focuses on building relationships and you will note that we indicate that 80 percent of your time should be invested in these activities while 20 percent invested in activities that build the firm's reputation.

Relationship building – invest 80% of your time in this area

Rule 1: People do business with people

Rule 2: People do business with people

Rule 3: People do business with people

This list is designed to provide firm owners with a gentle reminder regarding personal marketing responsibilities.

1. Contact A clients at least monthly

2. Contact your referral sources monthly

3. Contact your top five prospects bi-monthly

4. Research your prospects and their business and think of ways you can solve their problems or alert them to opportunities

5. Make your friends, family and social contacts aware of the firm's capabilities

6. Create a list of other professionals outside your firm who might be referral sources

7. Have someone else in the firm interview your clients

8. Send your clients, contacts and referral sources an article that might be of interest to them

9. Take someone to breakfast, lunch or dinner

10. Invite someone to a sporting or cultural event, or to play golf/tennis/squash etc.

11. Invite clients and referral sources to seminars

Relationship and reputation building

12. Send personal notes/emails of congratulations for accomplishments

13. Join organisations and networks that are meaningful to clients and referrals

14. Update your mailing list

15. Update your referral list – if you have not had a referral in the last six months then they are referring to someone else

16. Double your referral contacts

17. Add a PS to any standard letter accompanying a firm ambassador

18. Sign correspondence in ink – any colour other than black

19. Send birthday cards to *A* clients

20. Always thank those who refer

21. Be active in the community

22. Involve your staff as much as possible

23. Track your results

24. Think about ways you can expand services to clients

25. Introduce clients to your referrals

26. Develop a marketing plan for an individual client

27. Offer to help clients with project management and budgeting

28. Offer to help clients with a KPI plan.

Reputation building – invest 20% of your time in this area

Rule 1. Build your brand

Rule 2. Become a famous person

Rule 3. It's not who you know, it's who knows you

1. Identify three newsworthy matters that you can write an article or newswire about – check out www.newsnow.co.uk for ideas and research

Relationship and reputation building | 6th:4

2. Keep up-to-date with news in your niche service areas

3. Join an association that supports your speciality

4. Obtain the mailing list for group(s) in which you are involved

5. Make sure your biography is up-to-date and includes something personal

6. Speak when you can on your area of expertise

7. Send a letter to editors who might be interested in publishing articles prepared by you – include a list of topics for them to consider and then stay in touch and get to know them

8. Become more involved in industry groups related to your area of expertise

9. Make sure a press release is issued for your accomplishments

10. Make sure you are aware of conferences/seminars/trade shows to attend within your field of expertise. Offer to speak.

11. Look out for forthcoming events in your community that will provide you with an opportunity to meet people

12. Develop a 20 second infomercial about you and your firm

13. Attend a networking event

14. Make a list of the ways in which our practice is different from your competitors

6th session

Module 5
A range of marketing activities

In talking to those who attend marketing seminars I learn that for some just 'one good idea' is what they are looking for, that golden nugget or jewel in the crown moment. While I feel there is more to a marketing coaching session that this one moment of revelation, I thought that for those who still seek yet one more idea, I would devote this final coaching session to a few of the good ideas that I have either thought of myself or borrowed from others.

	Good ideas	
No.	**That one good idea**	**For you?**
1	**Be prepared to invest:** Marketing is intended to be part of the mix of client service. In fact, in my opinion we should spend more time marketing to clients than prospects. So what does it take? We have already spent some time looking at marketing, but before we delve into this final coaching session let's remind ourselves of what it takes. If are looking to grow your firm, stay ahead of inflation and replace clients lost through attrition you will probably need to have a new client fee target of up to and possibly more than 10 percent of your existing fees. That will need some resourcing and that includes financial and human. Our benchmark for year on year growth is three percent of gross fees and 200 hours for each owner.	
2	**Personal prospecting: Clients to die for:** Carry a card in your wallet/handbag with a list of the clients you would die to act for. Make sure this includes the client's name - not just the company name. If you do not have a name – you don't have a prospect. Remember after the second Iraq war how the American government issued picture cards of those they wished to apprehend? How about a file with pictures of the websites of your prospects?	
3	**Personal pointers:** Clothing. 90% of your appearance is your clothes. Be prepared to invest in your attire. Do you need to upgrade your wardrobe? John Molloy's book 'Dress for Success' was written over 30 years ago, but it's message is as relevant today as it was then. Dress for success! Your name badge. I never go anywhere without my own name badge. The badge is suitably branded and laminated and my name is in a large point size so that it can be read from a reasonable distance. There is nothing worse, in my opinion, than a name badge in 12 point that cannot be read unless you are close up.	

4	**Personal marketing plan (PMP): Every firm owner should have one:** Every accounting firm owner should have a personal plan. Who are your referrals (with more than one owner the referrals should encompass a greater number). Who are your prospects? What are your targets? What are your cross-serving goals? What are your strengths - how does the PMP maximise these?	
5	**Be famous:** What can you be famous for in your marketplace? Make yourself famous, stand above the crowd and you will win more business and be able to charge a higher rate for your services. What can you do to make yourself (even more) well known in your marketplace. What expertise can you acquire? How can you gain more clients in your area of expertise? Can you gain speaking engagements? Author articles? Write for a local newspaper. Be interviewed on radio or TV?	
6	**Great questions – What are yours?:** What are the 'killer' questions that will penetrate your client/prospects mind? Do you know how much money you will need to live on in retirement? Do you know what your competitors are doing? If you could change one thing about your business what would it be?	
7	**Owners – Take a risk and recommend your other partners!:** It is surprising how many firm owners do not recommend their other partners who have specialisms. If that is true in your firm why not gather round the table with your client lists and openly discuss where you could introduce another owner to one of the firm's (not yours) clients.	
8	**Business cards: Quality is important:** Make sure you have a supply in all your suits/outfits and include cards in your car and all your cases. Can you give your spouse/partner a supply? Include a personal mission statement or an indication of your service specialisation. Cards should be well designed and printed on good quality paper stock. Include your email address, direct dial and mobile contact details.	
9	**Business cards – Give or collect?:** It is more important to collect cards than to give your card away. When you give your card out you have no idea if the recipient will ever make contact. However if you ask a prospect for their card that confirms your interest in them and when you call you have the business card of a 'friend' which should help you when explaining the reason for your call to the receptionist. Many business cards include a mobile number, which so long as you ask, 'is now a convenient time to call' gives you direct access for any follow up contact. When you collect cards ask if you may add their name to your email database so you can 'keep then up to date with your news'. Some firms have a weekly or monthly newswire which can be used to keep in contact with prospects as well as clients.	

A range of marketing strategies that work

10	**Business cards – Make sure your staff have a card:** Everyone knows someone who would make a good client. Having a card is just one way everyone can affirm their value and provide a way of letting staff know that they are important and responsible for marketing.	
11	**Staff marketing – Include staff in your marketing:** Lead them – by example. Help them to overcome the fear of marketing. Be positive. Lead by walking the talk yourself. The eagle is thrown out of its nest by its parents in order to make it fly. You will probably have to adopt a similar approach as marketing is not most people's first choice activity! On the other hand if you can train them to be successful, success is habit forming. As their coach it is important they know the rules and that you are essentially playing to them. **Train them –** Encourage/require them to attend marketing seminars. Include them in new client meetings. Remember the Karate Kid and how Mr. Myagi trained Daniel for the All Valley Tournament? The coach passed on his skills to the next generation and trained him to be a winner. **Resource them –** Not just business cards, but give them the financial resources to take people out to lunch. How much? How about unlimited?! Staff are most unlikely to abuse the trust you place in them. **Inform them –** What are your plans? Give them a Key Card with details of the next quarter's marketing activities. What are the results of the marketing? What help are you looking for? Hold a marketing meeting every month. Let them know how important this is by holding this in firm time and not their time. If you do decide to hold meetings during the lunch hour, than maybe this could be half work time and half lunch time with lunch provided by the firm. **Reward them –** Make sure your schemes are written, clarifying the time period, who can qualify and at what level. Tell staff how they can meet their goals and how they will be measured. Staff will need to know what will be awarded to them and when. What is not included? What actions will not be allowed and what disclaimers may apply. People will do what they are rewarded for. An incentive scheme is a planned activity designed to motivate people to achieve predetermined organisational objectives. One favourite is the 10 percent of fee award – a real incentive is where this is given for maybe two or three years – or some firms give that reward on an ongoing basis while the employee remains. Another increasingly popular scheme is the marketing miles award scheme. However, let there not be too much emphasis on monetary reward for better than money is praise and personal gestures – those things that do not cost money are ironically often the most effective. **Achievability –** It is important to make your scheme simple, establishing realistic individual goals, making sure that your expectations are achievable. **Accountability –** Keep them accountable for what they are doing and their investment in the marketing process.	

12	**Extension services:** What extension services do you have that staff are best placed to identify? Maybe payroll, VAT, computerised accounting? Have your staff complete a review at the end of every job noting down those services from which the client might benefit.	
13	**Lost clients – Maybe you would like them back:** Retain them on your marketing database. Maybe after they have experienced their new accountant's service you could ask if they would meet with you over lunch and you could ask if they would be interested in returning as a client. They may have left and not found the new accountant is giving them the advice or service promised.	
14	**Tip board – In reception:** Include a tip board with ideas for tax saving, profit improvement, firm events and so on.	
15	**Surveys – What else can we do for you?:** Client surveys provide an opportunity to enquire if there is any service that the client is seeking.	
16	**Clients – Two key fee winning questions:** Remember not to overtly sell to clients rather use questions to probe needs so you can match your service solutions. "How else can we help you?

Do you know anyone else who needs a good (or great – dependent on your client relationship and your confidence!) accountant.
It is reported by some networks that 98% of clients are happy to recommend but that 97% have never been asked. It's not unprofessional to ask – it's just good business practice. | |
| 17 | **Mailshots – Make sure they are not junk mail:** No one believes they send junk mail, but somehow we all receive it. After years of ever-increasing email, maybe some like to receive a good quality newsletter or tax planning brochure that can be read at leisure. Make sure your mailings are personal and relevant. Here are a few recommendations:

1. Send a letter that is personally signed

2. Include a handwritten P.S. Make sure you use ink or a colour that makes it clear that this is not a computer-generated signature

3. Maybe write a margin note or highlight a section that you consider relevant to the recipient

4. Maybe highlight a section in the marketing piece of an article or paragraph that applies to the client/prospect.

Direct mail is intended to increase name recognition with prospects and potential referral sources. | |

A range of marketing strategies that work

18	**Give aways – It's always good to have something to give:** It may be a tax card or a pen. There is always a wide selection of give aways that you can peruse on the web. Looking for something with a little value? How about a memory stick? These should, of course, all have your branding.
19	**Give away a meeting – You surely have the time to be more visible?:** If you look at your time management, could you allow 50 hours a year for meeting with clients for free? This meeting will allow you to relax, get to know your client and ask questions. In my opinion it is impossible to spend an hour with a client and not identify areas where they need help. The only question is, can you help them? Remember, the dentist's receptionist example? You can use this (free) meeting to set up another (fee paying) meeting.
20	**Be a speaker:** Not on everyone's to do list, but...speaking provides a forum for introducing you, your firm and its skills. Choose topics that are relevant and interesting to your audience. What speaking opportunities are available to you?
21	**Your database:** I believe every firm should have a database of prospects. Who would you like to act for? How many should you have? Taking into account the cost of keeping the database up-to-date I would tend to err on the cautious side. My rule of thumb (and it is mine and not one that is borne out by extensive research) is that you should have 50 prospects for the firm and 50 for every owner. So if you have a three owner firm them you should seek a quality and relevant database of 200 prospects. Properly managed that database should yield one new client per owner every year.
22	**When something goes wrong – Problems sometimes lead to new business!:** Sometimes something happens that shouldn't, what do you do? I have found that if you handle these situations sensibly and promptly this often leads to additional business. Make sure you don't become defensive. Here are the big three rules: say... • We're sorry (empathy) • We're responsible (even if not at fault) • We'll fix it (action)
23	**Marketing culture:** You have a marketing culture when: • Your partners want to spend more money on marketing • Marketing meetings are attended by everyone who was scheduled to attend • Partners ask for help with their marketing • Partners ask, "how can I be more effective?" • Partners ask clients for referrals • Marketing takes place all year round • You invest in someone dedicated to marketing the firm

24	**Want to be outrageous?:** Here are a few ideas from firms who were: Indoor golf: Use indoor holes, water and sand bunkers and invite clients, referrals and prospects to bring their putters. The indoor golf finishes with lunch in your '19th' hole. Host your own TV programme? Sounds American? Yes, it certainly is, but this firm even had their Senator wanting to be interviewed on the local programme. Oktoberfest: Invite clients to come and taste a range of beers. Include raffles and provide taxis to take attendees home These are just a small selection of the ideas I gained as a member of the Association of Accounting Marketers, Kansas, USA	

Failure: As Henry Ford once said, "Failure is merely an opportunity to more intelligently begin again."

And finally...

You have reached the end of your coaching sessions. I trust you have found these of benefit. I would like to conclude by sharing with you some of the pearls of wisdom I have gleaned from those who have mentored me.

Firstly, my own thoughts. One day I turned my calculator on and worked out that I was going to live for about 600,000 hours – not a lot when you call it like that. So, I have always felt that I should be as much in charge of my life as I could. My Christian beliefs assure me that I will one day be in eternity, but until that day I seek to serve others and endeavour to enrich the lives of others. I have been lecturing on marketing and management for over 20 years and am thankful that accountants turn out and return to hear my thoughts and ideas on management. I trust you have found this programme useful, I know it contains insights and strategies which if you adapt them to your situation and ideas will help you improve your firm, your life and, I like to think, the lives of your staff and clients.

Here are some of the people I have met along life's path – my thanks to all of them:

Jerry Atkinson, CPA

Jerry is the founder of Atkinson's, the largest CPA firm in New Mexico. Apart from his friendship and his willingness to come to lecture for me in the UK, he taught me the importance of planning to be financially independent at the age of 55. He reckoned that he could tell anyone where to go if by the time he was 55 he had decided he had had enough. Some twenty years after I first met Jerry, I had sold all my businesses, and if I wanted to, could retire. Jerry? He left the firm to others but, I understand, still retains an office at Atkinsons.

Dave Cottle, CPA

Dave is the co-author of Clients 4Life and was a companion for over 10 years as we travelled around the country lecturing accountants on accounting firm management and marketing. What did Dave teach me? We spent probably a couple of hundred hours travelling and having meals together. We stretched each others intellect. He was able to gain from my varied experiences as a practitioner and my ability to think creatively. I benefited from having someone who would listen and always add value and insights. His experience is immense and his writing ability an art I learned to greatly respect.

Dr Gerry Faust

Gerry is a consultant based in San Diego. He was the founder of a 200 person company that he eventually sold to Andersen's. He was involved in training NASA astronauts and consulted with the White House and many well known global brands. He allowed me to work with him recording his management programmes, including Life Cycles and Driving to Prime. He taught me much and gave much in terms of his friendship and hospitality. From Gerry I learned all about 'change energy'.

There is a limit to what an organisation or an individual can implement. He suggested it is possible to make no more than 5-8 changes in a twelve month period. So, at the end of this programme do not contemplate implementing all those changes immediately.

Allan Koltin, CPA

Allan is the CEO of Practice Development Institute (PDI) in Chicago. PDI are a company similar to Practice Track as marketing publishers for the profession. Over ten years Allan and I exchanged ideas about publications and I became a member of the Profit Advisers group formed by PDI to train accountants in the art of profit improvement consulting.

Dr Bob Taylor

Bob was the President of Associated Accounting Firms International. His Association comprised 40 of the most prestigious firms in the USA. For over ten years Bob and his Vice President, Mike Platt invited me to attend and speak at their annual marketing partners and then their managing partners conferences. The managing partners' conferences provided such insights into the management of an accounting firm. I learned so much and was fortunate in having an accounting practice that I could implement what I learnt across the pond. My thanks to Bob for his willingness to allow me to stand alongside such accounting firm giants. Generosity was Bob's nature.

And a few others who have deposited their friendship and wisdom:

There are others, including August Aquila, Chuck Bentley, Sheila Buchanan, Peter Briscoe, Jean Carragher, Tracey Crevar-Warren, James Cross, Howard Dayton, Paul Dunn, Neil Elliott, Steve Fischer, Irwin Friedman, Leisa Gill, Sally Glick, Ben Heald, Pastor Johnny Hunt, Dave Jones, Dave Krajonowski, Gary Kravitz, Tim Levey, Ken McManus, David Pratt, Mike Platt, Barry Schimel, Lea Sloan, Henry South, James Stapleton, Bill and Ruth Swaim, Larry Wojick, and Will Womble, (but I am sure you have read enough.)

My thanks to all those who I have been able to spend time with – my clients, staff, family, friends and those in the accounting profession with whom I have spent time. I also have the Directors of Crown Financial Ministries to thank for giving me the opportunity to continue writing and building an organisation to help people with their finances.